HISTORICAL NOTES
ON
GERMAN DIVISIONS.
PART 1

ACTIVE DIVISIONS
ENGAGED ON THE BRITISH FRONT
IN FRANCE UP TO JANUARY, 1918

The Naval & Military Press Ltd

Published by
The Naval & Military Press Ltd
5 Riverside, Brambleside, Bellbrook
Industrial Estate, Uckfield, East Sussex,
TN22 1QQ England

Tel: +44 (0) 1825 749494
Fax: +44 (0) 1825 765701

www.naval–military-press.com
www.military-genealogy.com

[S.S. 642A.]   IA/47293.

PRESS A—6/18—5915S—750.

HISTORICAL NOTES ON GERMAN DIVISIONS ENGAGED ON THE BRITISH FRONT IN FRANCE UP TO JANUARY, 1918.

PART I.

ACTIVE DIVISIONS.

GENERAL STAFF (INTELLIGENCE),
GENERAL HEADQUARTERS.
May, 1918.

INDEX.

ACTIVE DIVISIONS.

HISTORICAL NOTES ON GERMAN DIVISIONS.

NOTE ON THE GUARD CORPS (1st and 2nd GUARD DIVISIONS.)

Composition. The Guard Corps, which is recruited from the whole of Prussia and from Alsace-Lorraine, consists of the 1st and 2nd Guard Divisions. The headquarters of the Corps and both divisions are in Berlin, as are also the depôts of all the infantry regiments composing them, except that of the 1st Foot Guards, which is at Potsdam.

The composition of the Guard Corps, when it took the field, was as follows :—The 1st Guard Division consisted of the 1st Guard Infantry Brigade (1st and 3rd Foot Guards Regiments) and the 2nd Guard Infantry Brigade (2nd and 4th Foot Guards Regiments). The 2nd Guard Division consisted of the 3rd Guard Infantry Brigade (1st Guard Grenadier Regiment (Kaiser Alexander)) and 3rd Guard Grenadier Regiment (*Königin* Elisabeth) and the 4th Guard Infantry Brigade (2nd Guard Grenadier Regiment (Kaiser Franz) and 4th Guard Grenadier Regiment (*Königin* Augusta). The four Guard Grenadier Regiments are generally known by the names of the sovereigns after whom they are called.

The Guard Corps retained its four-regiment organization until the beginning of 1916, when the 5th Guard Division was formed. To form the new division, the 3rd Foot Guards Regiment was withdrawn from the 1st Guard Division, which also detached the staff of the 2nd Guard Infantry Brigade, and the 3rd Guard Grenadier Regiment was transferred from the 2nd Guard Division. The staff of the 4th Guard Infantry Brigade was transferred to the 220th Division. The two divisions of the Guard Corps were thus reduced to three regiments each, grouped respectively under the 1st and 3rd Guard Infantry Brigades.

History, 1914. At the outbreak of war, the Guard Corps formed part of the Second Army under von Bülow, which entered France by way of Charleroi, on the left of the First Army, and marched southward by way of Rethel and Reims. In the battle of the Marne, it suffered severe casualties, being driven by the French into the marshes of St. Gond and losing heavily in prisoners and material.

When the " race for the sea " began, the Guard Corps was transferred to the Sixth Army under the Crown Prince of Bavaria. Early in November, a composite Guard Division, consisting of two regiments of Foot Guards and two regiments of Guard Grenadiers, was sent up to take part in the first battle of Ypres. It relieved the 54th Reserve Division about the 8th November, and on the 11th November took part in the great attack astride the Ypres—Menin road. The Guard suffered very heavy casualties in this attack. While advancing to the attack through the woods, they lost their direction and were enfiladed by machine guns, and subsequently a large number of them, who had forced their way right through the British lines, were cut off and all either killed or captured.

1915. Early in 1915, the 1st Guard Division was transferred to Champagne, and was severely engaged with the French in the Perthes—Beauséjour area. The 2nd Guard Division, which had returned to the Second Army some time before, remained in the Monchy—Hébuterne sector.

At the end of March, the Guard Corps was concentrated in Alsace, and was transported to Russia to take part in the great offensive of 1915. It fought throughout the campaign in Galicia and Poland in the Eleventh Army under von Mackensen, taking part in all the principal battles, and suffered heavy casualties. When in September, 1915, the Guard Corps left the Eleventh Army to be transferred to the Western front, von Mackensen sent a message to its Commander, General Freiherr von Plettenberg, reviewing the achievements of the Corps, which, he said, had formed the backbone of his army.

The Guard Corps arrived in Belgium about the 20th September. It was hurried up to meet the French attack on the 25th September in the Souchez area, and came into line on the 27th September. In this fighting the Corps did not cover itself with glory; a captured letter, indeed, declared that two regiments of the 2nd Guard Division had " for ever disgraced themselves in the eyes of the Emperor," and that no further decorations were to be given to these regiments. While these stories may have been exaggerated, there is no doubt that for some time after the Artois fighting the Guard was in disfavour; for nine months it remained in the quiet sector in front of Noyon, and not a single Guard formation (except the Guard Ersatz Division) took part in the battle of Verdun.

1916. The Guard Corps was transferred from Artois to the Noyon area towards the end of October, 1915, and remained there until the end of July, 1916. The 1st Guard Division was then relieved, and in mid-August appeared in line in the Clery sector, immediately north of the Somme. The 2nd Guard Division was not relieved until the 10th August, and came into line on the 25th in the Maurepas sector, on the right of the 1st Guard Division. Both divisions were in line for about a fortnight; although fairly heavily engaged, they suffered less severely than many divisions engaged in the Somme battle.

The Guard Corps now returned for a few weeks to the Oise area, but early in November the two divisions were in line again immediately south of the Somme, the 1st Guard Division holding the La Maisonette—Biaches sector with the 2nd Guard Division on its left, in the Barleux sector. They remained in line here until February, 1917, when the 1st Guard Division was relieved by the 56th Division and sent out to rest, while towards the end of the month the 2nd Guard Division moved north of the Somme and relieved the 29th Division. It was itself relieved during March, and went to join the 1st Guard Division in the Sissonne area.

When the French offensive on the Aisne was delivered on the 16th April, the 1st and 2nd Guard Divisions were immediately brought into line, to relieve divisions which had borne the brunt of the first onslaught. The 1st Guard Division relieved the 19th Reserve Division in the Cerny sector, south of Laon, while the 2nd Guard Division relieved the 5th Guard Division farther east, on the Vauclerc Plateau. They were most severely engaged in the second big French attack on the 5th May, when prisoners of all the regiments of both divisions were taken. The 1st and 2nd Guard Divisions were relieved on the 8th-9th May, and, after a short rest, put into line in quiet sectors in the Argonne. The survivors of the 2nd Guard Division were reviewed by the Crown Prince near Montcornet on the 14th May.

The 1st and 2nd Guard Divisions were relieved in the Argonne at the end of June, and on the 4th-5th July left for Galicia. The 2nd Guard Division entrained on the 4th July in the area north of Verdun, and travelled *viâ* Namur—Liége—Aachen—Düsseldorf—Minden—Hannover—Berlin—Frankfurt a/O.—Posen—Lodz—Warsaw Brest-Litovsk—Kovel—Lemberg to Oziduv, where it detrained on the 9th July. The 1st Guard Division entrained on the 5th July in the Sedan area, travelled *viâ* Namur—Liége—Aachen—Cologne—Cassel—Halle—Leipzig—Cottbus—Lissa—Ostrov—Lodz—Warsaw—Ivangorod—Kovel—Jaroslav—Lemberg, and detrained at Zloczov about the 11th July. The two divisions took part in the great German counter-offensive in Eastern Galicia. On the 25th-26th July in the presence of the Emperor, they crossed the Sereth near Tarnopol and stormed the heights on the eastern bank. The advance was not continued far east of Tarnopol, its maximum depth being attained farther south, where the frontier river, the Zbrucz, was reached. The 1st Guard Division remained in the Tarnopol area until the end of August, while the 2nd Guard Division was transferred for a short time to the Koudrintz sector, north of the Dniester.

At the end of August, the two divisions were transferred to the Riga front, and took part in the equally successful offensive which began there on the 1st September.

It should be noted that the Guard Corps Staff did not accompany the two divisions to the Eastern front. During September it was in command of the Ypres Group, in Flanders.

The two divisions now parted company for a time. The 2nd Guard Division entrained about the 10th September at Zanke, travelled *viâ* Mitau—Kovno—Schneidemühl—Bromberg—Posen—Berlin—Hannover—Düsseldorf—Aachen—Liége—Namur—Charleville, and detrained at Tournes (near the last-named place) about the 16th September. At the beginning of October, it went into line south of Laon, in the Malmaison sector. Here it was overwhelmed and practically annihilated in the French attack of the 23rd October. Its losses during the preliminary bombardment were very heavy, and over 1,700 prisoners of the division were taken in the attack. Its total casualties are estimated to have amounted to over 80 per cent. of establishment. On its withdrawal from the Aisne front, the division went into line in the quiet St. Mihiel sector, and remained there till the 11th January, 1918, when it was relieved by the 201st Division and went to rest in the Charleville area.

The 1st Guard Division did not leave Russia until October. It entrained about the 16th October near Riga, travelled *viâ* Königsberg—Posen—Halle—Cassel—Coblenz—Sedan, and detrained near Rethel about the 21st October. It relieved the 14th Reserve Division in the Beine sector (east of Reims) on the 25th October, and remained there till the 22nd January, 1918. It was then relieved by the 203rd Division, and went to join the 2nd Guard Division in the Charleville area.

The Guard Corps has an immense reputation. In peace time, of course, it was the crack German Corps, and drew its officers entirely from the Prussian aristocracy. It has, nevertheless, had a somewhat chequered career in the present war, and though it seems to have recovered from the loss of *moral* and prestige from which it suffered in the autumn of 1915, its divisions are to-day no better fighting units than many others which do not wear " Litzen." The recent employment of the 1st and 2nd Guard Divisions in the easy and spectacular successes on the Russian front was probably designed to stimulate their fighting spirit and restore their ancient prestige.

Guard Corps ...	...	Gen. d. Kav. Graf. zu Dohna-Schlobitten.
1st Guard Division	...	Col. Prinz Eitel Friedrich.
2nd Guard Division	...	Maj.-Gen. v. Friedeburg.

NOTE ON THE 3rd GUARD DIVISION.

The 3rd Guard Division originally formed the Guard Reserve Corps with the 1st Guard Reserve Division. It was then, like all other German divisions, organized in two brigades of two regiments: the 5th Foot Guards and 5th Guards Grenadiers formed the 5th Guard Infantry Brigade, and the Guard Fusilier and *Lehr* Regiments the 6th Guard Infantry Brigade.

History,
1914.
 The Guard Reserve Corps was originally ordered to the Western front, but was turned back at Namur on the 27th August, 1914, and transported *via* East Prussia to Silesia, whence it took part in the invasion of Southern Poland. The Army Group of which it formed part was outflanked and compelled to retire on Lodz. In November, it was transferred to the Ninth Army under von Mackensen, and in the following month to the Tenth. It took part in the severe fighting on the Bzura in the winter of 1914-1915.

1915.
 Early in 1915, the Corps was dissolved and the 3rd Guard Division itself split up, the 5th Guard Brigade (5th Foot Guards Regiment and 5th Guard Grenadier Regiment) going north to East Prussia, and the 6th Guard Brigade (Guard Fusilier Regiment and *Lehr* Infantry Regiment) south to the Carpathians, where it was engaged in the region of the Uzsok Pass.

In March, 1915, the 6th Guard Brigade was strengthened by the addition of the 9th Grenadiers from the 3rd Division, and henceforth these three regiments formed the 3rd Guard Division; the two regiments of the 5th Guard Brigade joined the new 4th Guard Division.

The 3rd Guard Division formed part of General von Linsingen's Army in the great summer campaign of 1915. It marched through the Carpathians to Stryj, fought its way eastward through the hilly wooded region of Eastern Galicia, across the Gnila Lipa and Zlota Lipa, and, when the southern or pivot wing of the advance came to a standstill, took up its position west of Tarnopol. It remained here throughout the winter, and formed the " Korps Marschall " with the 48th Reserve Division—the German leaven in Bothmer's Army.

1916.
 The 3rd Guard Division was transferred to the Western front in April, 1916, and went into line in Champagne, where it was not seriously engaged. During this period it was reviewed at Vouziers by the Emperor, who delivered a characteristic address. At the beginning of June the Division went to rest at Valenciennes.

On the commencement of the Anglo-French offensive on the 1st July, the 3rd Guard Division was hurried to the Somme. It came into action in the Contal-maison—Bazentin-le-Petit sector on the 4th July, and remained in line as a division for twelve days (the Guard Fusiliers, which were engaged at Ovillers, four days longer). During this period it met the full weight of the British attack and suffered heavy losses.

The total casualties, admitted officially, for the 3rd Guard Division on the Somme were 5,174, or 57·5 per cent. of the establishment.

The 3rd Guard Division fought very well on the Somme in difficult conditions; its discipline and *moral* then left little to be desired.

On its withdrawal from the Somme, the division was sent into the trenches near Dixmude, and at the end of August was transferred to Galicia, where it was identified near Halicz. It entrained in the Bruges area between the 30th August and 3rd September and travelled *via* Liége—Cologne—Leipzig—Dresden—Cracow—Przemysl to Rohatyn (34 miles north of Stanislau).

At Halicz, the 3rd Guard Division took part in the German counter-offensive and again suffered severely. On the 24th November, it returned to the Western front. Entraining at Saruki-Dolne, the division travelled *via* Lemberg—Jaroslav—Görlitz—Dresden — Chemnitz — Hof — Nürnberg — Heilbronn — Bruchsal — Strassburg — Mülhausen to Rheinweiler, where it arrived on the 29th November. There it rested

1917.
 for a month till it went into line, early in January, in the Forêt de Parroy sector, east of Lunéville. The division remained in this quiet sector until the 6th April, when it was relieved by the 15th Bavarian Division. It entrained at Metz on the 8th April, and came by Montmédy—Sedan—Charleville to Cambrai.

In the British offensive at Arras, which commenced on the 9th April, the 3rd Guard Division was not engaged as a formed unit. On the 15th April, elements of the Guard Fusilier Regiment and *Lehr* Infantry Regiment took part in a temporarily successful counter-attack on Lagnicourt in support of the 2nd Guard Reserve Division. The 9th Grenadier Regiment, on the other hand, was sent to support the 3rd Bavarian Division in the Monchy-le-Preux sector, south-east of Arras, where the regiment was identified on the 24th April by prisoners. During May, the division saw some hard fighting around Bullecourt and lost over 200 prisoners to the British. It was withdrawn about the 18th May to the Cambrai area. After a short period of rest it returned to the Pronville—Inchy-en-Artois sector, where it replaced the 207th Division on the 1st-3rd June. Ten days later it extended its front and took over the sector of the 2nd Guard Reserve Division. It was withdrawn again on the 22nd June and, in anticipation of a British offensive in Flanders, was transferred to reserve in the Bruges area. The 1st Guard Reserve Division took its place in the Pronville sector.

The 3rd Guard Division entrained at Cambrai on the 9th July and travelled *via* Douai and Lille to Thourout. It rested in this area until the 29th July and then moved up *via* Staden to the Langemarck area. On the 30th July the division began to relieve the 23rd Reserve Division in the Pilkem sector. Early on the following day the great British infantry attack caught both divisions in the middle of the relief and routed them. The 3rd Guard Division suffered extremely heavy losses, leaving over

1,000 prisoners in the hands of the British. It was relieved on the 5th-6th August by the 79th Reserve Division and transferred almost immediately to Alsace.

After several weeks in line and a period of rest in Alsace the division entrained at Blotzheim on the 1st October and travelled *via* Schlettstadt and Sedan to Juniville, in Champagne. It remained there until the 9th October, when it was transported to Flanders, detraining at Ingelmunster, and relieved the 233rd Division east of Zonnebeke on the 16th October. The division held this sector till the 19th October and again from the 26th October—1st November, when it was withdrawn to rest in the area north-east of Ghent.

When the British offensive at Cambrai was delivered on the 20th November the 3rd Guard Division was rushed up to this area and relieved the 214th Division on the 22nd November in the Bourlon sector. In the subsequent fighting for Bourlon village the division acquitted itself well, but suffered very heavy losses. It was with-

1918. drawn to rest in the Valenciennes area early in December. On the 6th January, 1918, the division came into line west of Cambrai, astride the Bapaume road, relieving the 21st Reserve Division, and, after an uneventful month in line, was replaced by the 119th Division.

General. The 3rd Guard Division can be described as a good fighting unit. It has seen a great deal of hard fighting, in which it has usually acquitted itself well. At Ypres, in July, 1917, the *moral* of the men was not good and, in consequence, the division showed very little fight.

Maj.-Gen. von Roeder commands the 3rd Guard Division.

NOTE ON THE 4th GUARD DIVISION.

Composition. The 4th Guard Division was formed on the Russian front in March, 1915. Two of its regiments, the 5th Foot Guards and 5th Guard Grenadiers, were drawn from the 3rd Guard Division, while the 93rd Reserve Infantry Regiment came from the 1st Guard Reserve Division.

History, 1915. During the summer of 1915 the 4th Guard Division and the 1st Guard Reserve Division were engaged in the operations north of the Vistula and fought side by side in von Gallwitz's Army. About the middle of September both divisions, after fighting in the Smorgon—Vichniev area, were withdrawn from front line.

Early in October, 1915, the 4th Guard Division marched to Kovno, where it entrained on the 10th for France. It travelled *via* Königsberg—Lübeck—Hamburg—Aachen—Namur and detrained at Douai. The 1st Guard Reserve Division also came to France, and both divisions went into rest billets on the banks of the Scheldt.

1916. During January and February, 1916, the 4th Guard Division was engaged in digging in the Wytschaete—Messines area, and occasionally took over a sector of the front. When not so occupied, it underwent training in the Cambrai area. It was now combined with the 1st Guard Reserve Division to form the Guard Reserve Corps, under the command of General der Kavallerie Freiherr von Marschall. The two divisions were attached to units in various sectors of the Sixth Army front with a view to their being used eventually in active operations.

At the beginning of May, 1916, the corps came into line on the Arras front. The 4th Guard Division relieved the 1st Bavarian Division north-east of Neuville St. Vaast.

At the end of July the Guard Reserve Corps was transferred to the French front south of the Somme. The 4th Guard Division relieved the 18th Division in the Estrées sector, and was heavily engaged. On the 19th-20th August the Corps was withdrawn to Cambrai, and a few days later came into line in the Thiepval area. The 4th Guard Division took over the line from south of Thiepval to just west of Mouquet Farm, where it was engaged in hard local fighting. It was withdrawn on the 8th September and transferred to the Ypres salient, relieving the 51st Reserve Division north of Ypres about the middle of the month.

After an uneventful stay in the Ypres salient the Guard Reserve Corps returned to the Somme front and took over the Warlencourt sector from the XIX. Corps about the 5th November. The conditions, after some local fighting in November, approximated to those of ordinary trench warfare, and the corps was able to remain in line throughout the winter.

The 4th Guard Division suffered very heavy losses in the battle of the Somme. It reported casualties amounting to 76 per cent. for the period between July and November.

1917. The 4th Guard Division took part in the first stage of the retreat to the Hindenburg Line. About the middle of March it was withdrawn and went to rest in the Tournai area, where it remained until the 11th April, when it marched up *via* St. Amand, Orchies and Douai, and relieved the 16th Bavarian Division south of Lens. The division was not seriously engaged in this sector, but suffered fairly heavy losses from local enterprises and shelling. On about the 28th June it extended its front northwards, and on the 11th July was relieved by the 36th Reserve Division.

The 4th Guard Division rested in the Pont à Vendin and Meurchin area until the 15th August, and was then rushed up to the sector north of Lens to relieve the bulk of the 7th Division, which had been driven from its position by Canadian troops and had lost Hill 70. The 4th Guard Division made several unsuccessful attempts to recover the ground. It attacked in twelve waves, and had very heavy losses; over 700 men of the division were buried at Carvin.

About the middle of September, the 4th Guard Division was relieved north of Lens by the 39th Division and transported to the Ypres front. It entrained on the 23rd-24th September at Carvin and travelled *via* Lille—Roulers—Thourout to Wynendaele, arriving on the same day. The division remained in this area, in Army reserve, under the orders of the Dixmude Group, until the 26th September, when it was alarmed and brought to Moorslede. It came into line east of Zonnebeke on the 27th September, and relieved the 236th Division and elements of the 234th Division and 3rd Reserve Division. The 5th Foot Guard Regiment was ordered to make an attack on the 2nd October, but was unable to carry out the order owing to the demoralization caused by the British artillery fire. On the 4th October another attempt was made to launch this attack. The 4th Guard Division, assisted by elements of the 45th Reserve Division, were to attack on the front of the division and endeavour to retake the high ground lost in the successful British attack of the 26th September. This attack was, however, again frustrated. A British attack, ordered for the same day, forestalled it by ten minutes and completely annihilated the waiting troops. A captured document shows that the 93rd Reserve Infantry Regiment had extraordinarily heavy losses, and many men fled in the direction of Becelaere, ostensibly by orders of their commanders. Nothing could hold them. The 4th Guard Division suffered casualties amounting to 70 per cent. of its establishment and left 856 prisoners in the hands of the British.

Completely exhausted, the division was relieved by the 233rd Division and transferred to the St. Quentin area, where it replaced the 40th Division in a quiet sector south of Itancourt on the 14th October. At the end of December, the division was relieved by the 103rd Division and went to rest at Origny, where it underwent a course of training. On the 4th February, the 4th Guard Division came into line in the Pontruet sector (north of St. Quentin), relieving elements of the 206th Division, and, after four uneventful weeks in line, was relieved by the 208th Division.

General.

The 4th Guard Division can be classed among the good German divisions. It has usually done well, but, in the heavy fighting of 1917, at Lens and at Ypres, it was allotted such difficult tasks that its losses were far heavier than the results warranted.

The 4th Guard Division is commanded by Major-General Graf Finck von Finckenstein.

NOTE ON THE 5th GUARD DIVISION.

Composition.

The 5th Guard Division was formed early in February, 1917, in the St. Quentin area by regrouping. It comprises the 3rd Foot Guards Regiment (from 1st Guard Division), the 3rd Guard Grenadier Regiment (from 2nd Guard Division), and the 20th Infantry Regiment (from the 212th Division), which are grouped in the 2nd Guard Infantry Brigade.

History,
1917.

The 5th Guard Division first appeared in line towards the end of March west of Craonne, where it reinforced the front in anticipation of a French attack. On the 16th April, the division met the full weight of the French attack, and lost heavily. It was replaced by the 2nd Guard Division on the 19th April, and, after a short period of rest, relieved the 13th Landwehr Division on the River Ailette. The 5th Guard Division held this quiet sector until the 5th June, when it was replaced by the 211th Division and rested for a month. On the 9th July, the division relieved the 15th Division near Hurtebise on the Chemin des Dames, and carried out a series of costly attacks on the Californie Plateau between the 19th and 22nd July. The division was replaced almost at once by the 52nd Division, and then took over a quiet sector north of Aizy (Laon area) from the 43rd Reserve Division. On the 23rd October, it bore the brunt of the successful French attack on the River Ailette, and, although its losses in prisoners only amounted to about 300, the losses of some units of the division amounted to over 80 per cent. of the establishment.

After about a month's rest in the Vervins area, the 5th Guard Division came into line in the Vendhuille—Bellicourt sector, where it relieved the 183rd Division on the 30th November. The division saw no fighting in this sector, and was only identified by contact on two occasions. It was relieved by the 9th Bavarian Reserve Division on the 30th December, and went to rest in the Fourmies area, where it underwent a course of training.

General.

The 5th Guard Division has only been in line opposite British troops on one occasion, when it was not engaged in any infantry fighting. Judging from its composition, however, it should be a good fighting formation.

The 5th Guard Division is commanded by Maj.-Gen. von der Osten.

NOTE ON THE 4th DIVISION.

Composition. The 4th Division is recruited in the II. Army Corps District (Stettin). It originally consisted of the 7th Infantry Brigade (14th and 149th Infantry Regiments) and 8th Infantry Brigade (49th and 140th Infantry Regiments). It retained its four-regiment organization until September, 1916, when the 149th Infantry Regiment was transferred to the 213th Division and the staff of the 7th Brigade to the 222nd Division.

History, 1914. At the outbreak of war the 4th Division, with the 3rd Division, formed the II. Army Corps in the First German Army under von Kluck. It advanced on Paris viâ Hasselt, Aerschot, Brussels, Peruvelz, Cambrai, Morval, Le Transloy, Bray, sacked and burnt Senlis, and, on reaching St. Augustin (south-east of Paris) on the 5th September, 1914, was forced to retire, marching in a north-westerly direction. Turning north-east at Etavigny, the 4th Division was engaged and defeated by the French at Villers-Cotterets, and did not come to a standstill until it had reached the River Aisne.

Early in November, the 4th Division was transferred to Flanders, and took part in the first battle of Ypres. It was engaged in the area north of Menin from the 9th to the 22nd November.

Towards the end of 1914, the II. Corps was transferred to Russia and broken up. The 4th Division joined the Ninth Army under von Mackensen, and took part in the **1915.** winter fighting of the Bzura and Rawka. In February, it was transferred to the German Southern Army under von Linsingen in the Eastern Carpathians, and fought at Tucholka.

In April, 1915, the 4th Division was again placed under von Mackensen, now in command of the Eleventh Army in Galicia, and, in company with the Guard Corps, X. Corps and other German troops, took part in the great attack on the River Dunajec, which opened the summer campaign of 1915. During these operations the division formed part of a composite corps under von der Marwitz. It took part in the recapture of Przemysl and the advance on the line of the Bug, which compelled the Russians to retire to the Pripet marshes. In the middle of September, the 4th Division was north of Pinsk, in the Baranovitchi area.

The Allied offensive in the West, however, compelled the Germans to bring reinforcements from Russia. The 4th Division entrained on the 5th October at Brest Litovsk, travelled viâ Kalisch—Ostrovo—Lissa—Leipzig—Eisenach—Frankfurt-on-Main—Mainz—Diedenhofen—Sedan, and detrained at Charleville on the 9th October. About the 29th October, it went into line at Tahure, but was withdrawn a few days later and took up a position in the Reims sector, where it remained throughout the winter.

1916. Towards the end of April, 1916, the 4th Division was transferred viâ Rethel—Charleville—Sedan to the Stenay area. At the beginning of May, it came into line on the left bank of the Meuse, and took part in the attacks of the 4th May and following days in the Côte 304 area. It suffered very heavy losses, and on its relief by the 38th Division about the 12th May went to rest for two months in the Sedan area. The division returned to the battle-front about the 13th July, and was heavily engaged in the Thiaumont—Fleury sector, east of the Meuse. On the 3rd August, it returned to the left bank of the Meuse, where it held the quiet Avocourt sector until October. It then went to rest in the Spincourt area. After the successful French attack on the 15th-16th December, which resulted in the capture of the Côte du Poivre, Louvemont and Bézonvaux, it came into line in the Bézonvaux—Damloup sector, relieving the severely handled 39th Bavarian Reserve Division. It remained in this sector until April, 1917, but was not seriously engaged.

The 4th Division was one of the divisions which suffered most heavily in the Verdun battle. Its twelve battalions reported 10,201 casualties, a percentage of 85 per cent. of establishment. The losses sustained by the individual regiments were as follows :—

	Officers.		O.R.		Total.		Percentage of Establishment.
14th Inf. Regt. ...	50	...	2,560	...	2,610	...	87
149th Inf. Regt. ...	34	...	2,033	...	2,067	...	68·9
49th Inf. Regt. ...	60	...	2,454	...	2,514	...	83·8
140th Inf. Regt. ...	66	...	3,044	...	3,110	...	103·7

1917. On the 15th-16th April, 1917, the 4th Division was brought to the Reims sector to meet the French attack. It was relieved on the 4th May, but came into line again a week later in the Linguet sector (north-east of Reims). Early in June, it was transferred to Champagne, and engaged from the 6th-18th June in the Nauroy—Moronvilliers sector. After a month's rest, it returned to the front line in this area on the 17th July, and remained there till the end of October, when it was relieved by the 7th Reserve Division and 23rd Division, extending their fronts. The division travelled by rail from Juniville to Aerseele, arrived at Roulers on the 4th November, and came into line on the night of the 4th-5th November in the sector south-east of Poelcappelle, relieving elements of the 5th Bavarian Reserve and 111th Divisions. Its casualties on this front were heavy. The 14th Infantry Regiment, on arrival, suffered casualties from British artillery fire at Roulers station. In the successful attack, carried out by the Canadians on the 6th November, which culminated in the capture of Passchendaele, the 4th Division, although only on the flank of the attack, suffered very heavy losses.   On the night of the 10th-11th November, the 4th Division was replaced by the 199th Division, and was withdrawn to close support until the 16th November, when it returned to its old sector south-east of Poelcappelle.   Finally, on the 23rd November, the 4th Division was again replaced by the 199th Division and withdrawn for a short period of rest on the Belgian—Dutch frontier.   The division appeared in line again on the 30th November in a quiet sector opposite Armentières, and relieved the 2nd Guard Reserve Division.   On the 23rd January, 1918, it was relieved by the 42nd Division, and during February took part in manœuvres on a large scale in the Deynze area.

1918.

General.

The 4th Division is of average quality.   In the recent fighting at Ypres it did not distinguish itself, but showed a stubborn defence.

The 4th Division is commanded by Lieut.-Gen. Freyer.

NOTE ON THE 5th DIVISION.

Composition.

The 5th Division, which is recruited in the III. Army Corps District (Brandenburg), has its Headquarters at Frankfurt a/O.   The principal towns in the III. Army Corps District are Berlin, Frankfurt a/O., Brandenburg a/H., Cottbus, Spandau, Cüstrin, etc.

At the outbreak of war, the 5th Division consisted of the 9th Infantry Brigade (8th Body Grenadiers and 48th Infantry Regiment) and the 10th Infantry Brigade (12th Grenadiers and 52nd Infantry Regiment).   In March, 1915, the 48th Infantry Regiment was withdrawn to join the newly-formed 113th Division.

History, 1914.

In August, 1914, the III. Army Corps (5th and 6th Divisions) formed part of the First German Army under General von Kluck.   It took part in the battle of Charleroi, the march on Paris, the battle of the Marne, and the retreat to the Aisne, on which river it was engaged with the British Army.   On the commencement of trench warfare, the corps took up its position between the Oise and the Aisne, and remained

1915.

there until June, 1915, when it was relieved by the VIII. Army Corps.   The III. Corps now left the First Army.   On the 1st July, 1915, it was transported to Douai and, after a short spell in front line before Arras, went into rest billets, the 5th Division at Valenciennes, the 6th Division at Cambrai.

The Corps was now temporarily dissolved.   The 6th Division went to Serbia, while the 5th Division was sent to the Champagne front to reinforce on the opening of the French offensive in September, 1915.   It remained in this area for several weeks, and was then withdrawn to the Montmédy area to rest.

1916.

The 6th Division returned from Serbia in December, and the III. Army Corps reassembled in the Hirson—Sedan—Vouziers area.   During January and early in February, 1916, the Corps proceeded by stages to the Damvillers—Spincourt area.

On the 22nd February, the first great attack on the Verdun front was delivered. The III. Corps, with all its regiments in line, attacked on a front extending from the western edge of the Herbebois to the eastern slopes of the Côtes de Meuse.   It captured the Herbebois and the woods of La Vauche and Hassoule, and on Saturday, the 26th February, the German General Staff announced that " the 24th Brandenburg Infantry Regiment has taken by storm the armoured fort of Douaumont, the north-eastern pillar of the Verdun defences."   This success, however, was not developed ; the Germans held the fort, but the violent attacks made by the III. Corps on Douaumont village from the 28th February to 2nd March were all repulsed with heavy loss.

On the 2nd March, the Corps was withdrawn from front line to reorganize, but on the 8th March it reappeared, and delivered a series of violent attacks on the front from Douaumont village to the Hardaumont work.   It made small progress and again suffered heavy losses.   The Corps was then withdrawn for a longer period of rest and reorganization, the 5th Division going to the Saargemünd—Zabern region and the 6th Division to the neighbourhood of Mülhausen.

On the 28th-29th April and 6th-7th May, the III. Corps attacked in the Caillette Wood sector, immediately south of Fort Douaumont, and lost heavily for the third time.   At the end of May, it was withdrawn from the Verdun front.

The losses sustained at Verdun by the 19 infantry battalions of the III. Corps, as reported in the German casualty lists between the 15th March and 15th July, amount to 19,142 (over 100 per cent.).   The nine battalions of the 5th Division lost 9,161 (102 per cent.) and the 10 battalions of the 6th Division (including the 3rd *Jäger* Battalion) lost 9,981 (practically 100 per cent.).   The following table shows the losses of the individual regiments : —

	Officers.		O.R.		Total.		Percentage.
5th Division :							
8th Body Grenadier Regt.	54	...	3,256	...	3,310	...	110·3
12th Grenadier Regt.	64	...	2,920	...	2,984	...	99·5
52nd Infantry Regt.	56	...	2,985	...	3,041	...	101·4
	174	...	9,161	...	9,335	...	103·7

The 5th Division rested in the neighbourhood of Mörchingen in Lorraine until the beginning of the Allied offensive on the Somme. The division was then brought up *via* Metz—Namur—Charleroi to Valenciennes, thence to St. Quentin, and came into line in the Longueval—Delville Wood sector about the 21st July, relieving the 24th Reserve Division. It was severely engaged during the fortnight for which it remained in line, and casualties amounting to over 50 per cent. of its establishment have been reported. The division was relieved about the 5th August by the 26th Division and transferred to Champagne, where it relieved Fortmüller's Division in the Auberive sector.

Early in October, the 5th Division was relieved in the Auberive sector by the 53rd Reserve Division and came by Charleville—Sedan—Longuyon to the Verdun area, where it trained until the 31st October. On the 18th October, it was reviewed by the Emperor, accompanied by the Crown Prince, at Mercy-Le-Bas. On the 1st November, the 5th Division came into line on the Verdun front, in the Vaux sector, where the 9th Division had been pressed back by the French advance. Fighting having subsided, the division was relieved by the 39th Bavarian Reserve Division on the 14th December, and came to the Mülhausen area to rest.

1917. The 5th Division rested in Alsace throughout the winter of 1916-1917, and was not called upon to take part in any battle until April, when the French opened their offensive in Champagne. The division came into line south of Moronvilliers (Champagne) on the 20th April, four days after the opening of the battle, and came in for some extremely heavy fighting, losing a large number of prisoners to the French. It was replaced by the 33rd Division on the 3rd May, and withdrawn to the Conflans—Briey area (Woëvre) to rest.

Early in July, the 5th Division was transferred to Galicia, and took part in the German counter-offensive, which began on the 19th July, and culminated in the capture of Tarnopol, Trembowla and Czernowitz. The 5th Division was engaged in the area south of Tarnopol, and had reached the Skalat area on the Russian frontier by the 1st August. The losses of the division were not light in this fighting. A captured German letter shows that on the 23rd and 24th July the Russians delivered a series of counter-attacks, sometimes attacking in 16 waves, and inflicted severe casualties on the 5th Division.

Towards the end of September, when the fighting had ceased, the 5th Division was relieved by the 6th Reserve Division and, in October, was transferred to the Italian front. It left Russia on the 23rd and arrived in the Laibach area at the end of the month. While in Italy, the 5th Division was grouped under the III. Corps Staff. It took part in the fighting on the Tagliamento, the Brandenburger being singled out for praise in the German communiqué of the 1st November. The Division held the sector N.E. of Latisana on the lower course of the river. At the end of November, the 5th Division was holding the front before Monte Spinoncia, and on the 12th December took part together with the 4th Austrian Division in an attack against the Col della Berretta and Monte Spinoncia. It remained here until **1918.** the end of the year, when it was transferred to France, being identified in the neighbourhood of Vouziers during January, 1918.

General. The 5th Division has a great reputation. It has always been considered as one of the crack German Divisions. Its fighting value, however, has suffered as a result of its heavy losses at Verdun. Practically the whole of its fine officers' corps have been killed or disabled, and the reserve officers who have filled the gaps do not possess the confidence of their men. The division is composed almost entirely of Brandenburger, who are well known for their dash and vigour.

The *moral* of the 5th Division, which has been seriously engaged in 1917, is probably not up to its normal standard.

The 5th Division is commanded by Lieut.-Gen. von Wedel.

NOTE ON THE 6th DIVISION.

Composition. The 6th Division, which is recruited in the III. Army Corps District, has its Headquarters at Brandenburg a/H. The principal towns in the III. Corps District are Berlin, Frankfurt a/O., Brandenburg a/H., Cottbus, Spandau, Cüstrin.

At the beginning of the war, the 6th Division consisted of the 11th Infantry Brigade (20th and 35th Fusilier Regiments) and the 12th Infantry Brigade (24th and 64th Infantry Regiments). In March, 1915, the 35th Fusilier Regiment was transferred to the 56th Division. The three remaining regiments were grouped together in the 12th Infantry Brigade. This constitution remained until, in the autumn of 1916, the 20th Infantry Regiment was transferred to the new 212th Division, its place being taken by the 396th Regiment, which was formed by withdrawing companies from other regiments in the III. Corps.

History, 1914. In August, 1914, the III. Army Corps formed part of the First German Army under von Kluck. It took part in the battle of Charleroi, the march on Paris, the battle of the Marne and the retreat to the Aisne, on which river it was engaged with the British Army. On the commencement of trench warfare, the Corps took up its position between the Oise and the Aisne and remained there till June, 1915, when **1915.** it was relieved by the VIII. Corps. The III. Corps now left the First Army. On

1st July, 1915, it was transported to Douai and, after a short spell in front line before Arras, went into rest billets, the 5th Division at Valenciennes, the 6th Division at Cambrai.

The Corps was now temporarily dissolved. The 5th Division was sent to the Champagne front to reinforce on the opening of the French offensive in September, 1915, while the 6th Division went to Serbia. It entrained at Cambrai on 23rd September, and after a journey of five days *viâ* Sedan—Stuttgart—Munich—Vienna—Budapest arrived at Arad, in Southern Hungary. It was now grouped with the 25th Reserve Division in a temporary III. Army Corps. The 6th Division crossed the Danube at Semendria on the 9th October and took part in the advance up the valley of the Morava towards Kragujevatz. In the fighting between the 12th and 16th October, it is said to have suffered considerable losses. On the fall of Kragujevatz, the division was recalled to France. It entrained at Nagybecsekek on the 1st December, travelled *viâ* Budapest—Kättowitz—Breslau—Dresden—Frankfurt—Cologne—Liége—Namur to Fourmies, and went into rest billets in the Hirson area.

The III. Army Corps now reassembled in the Hirson—Sedan—Vouziers area. Early in February, the 6th Division entrained in the Hirson — Avesnes area and travelled *viâ* Arlon—Longwy to the neighbourhood of Spincourt, the 5th Division being by this time in the Damvillers area.

1916. On the 22nd February, the first great attack on the Verdun front was delivered. The III. Corps, with all its regiments in line, attacked on a front extending from the western edge of the Herbebois to the eastern slopes of the Côtes de Meuse. It captured the Herbebois and the woods of La Vauche and Hassoule, and on Saturday, the 26th February the German General Staff announced that " the 24th Brandenburg Infantry Regiment has taken by storm the armoured fort of Douaumont, the north-eastern pillar of the Verdun defences." This success, however, was not developed; the Germans held the fort, but the violent attacks made by the III. Corps on Douaumont village from the 28th February to the 2nd March were all repulsed with heavy loss.

On the 2nd March, the Corps was withdrawn from front line to reorganize, but on the 8th March it reappeared and delivered a series of violent attacks on the front from Douaumont village to the Hardaumont work. It made small progress and again suffered heavy losses. The Corps was then withdrawn for a longer period of rest and reorganization, the 5th Division going to the Saargemünd—Zabern region, and the 6th Division to the neighbourhood of Mülhausen i/E.

On the 28th-29th April and the 6th-7th May the III. Corps attacked in the Caillette Wood sector, immediately south of Fort Douaumont, and lost heavily for the third time. At the end of May it was withdrawn from the Verdun front.

The losses sustained at Verdun by the 19 infantry battalions of the III. Corps, as reported in the German casualty lists between the 15th March and the 15th July, amount to 19,142 (over 100 per cent.). The 9 battalions of the 5th Division lost 9,161 (102 per cent.), and the 10 battalions of the 6th Division (including the 3rd *Jäger* Battalion) lost 9,981 (practically 100 per cent.). The following table shows the losses of the individual regiments :—

5th Division—	Officers.	O.R.	Total.	Percentage.
8th Body Grenadier Regt....	54	3,256	3,310	110·3
12th Grenadier Regt. ...	64	2,920	2,984	99·5
52nd Infantry Regt. · ...	56	2,985	3,041	101·4
6th Division—				
20th Infantry Regt. ...	52	2,755	2,807	93·2
24th Infantry Regt. ...	58	2,680	2,738	90·1
64th Infantry Regt. ...	57	2,827	2,884	96·1
3rd *Jäger* Battalion ...	31	1,347	1,378	137·8
	372	18,770	19,142	(average) 104·1

In the middle of June, the 6th Division was transferred to Champagne and occupied quiet sectors, first north-east of Prunay and then east of Auberive. It was relieved by degrees during September, and, after resting in the Noyon region, came into line on 8th October and the following days north of the Somme, in the Gueudecourt sector, relieving elements of the 6th Bavarian Reserve Division and the 7th Reserve Division.

1917. The 6th Division was relieved in the Gueudecourt sector towards the end of October by the 23rd Reserve Division and was sent to the Argonne. Here it held a quiet sector of the line for a time, moving down later to Alsace, where it remained resting in the Mülhausen area until the French offensive in Champagne in April. Coming from Alsace, the 6th Division detrained at Ville-sur-Retourne on the 18th, proceeding to Pont Favarger and thence into line south of Moronvillers. The 5th Division, arriving on this front almost at the same time, held the sector on the right of the 6th. Both divisions were engaged in very heavy fighting, losing large numbers of prisoners and killed.

The 6th Division continued in line until the 3rd May, and was then relieved by the 10th Ersatz Division. It went back to rest in the neighbourhood of Mülhausen remaining in Alsace until July. It was then transferred to Russia, taking part in the big German counter offensive, which began on the 19th July and resulted in the capture of Tarnopol, Trembowla and Czernowitz. The 6th Division is known to have suffered heavy losses in Russian counter-attacks at the end of July. Early in October, the 6th Division was relieved by the 14th Bavarian Division, and entrained south-east of Tarnopol on the 9th. It travelled *via* Lemberg—Cracow—Dresden—Halle—Cassel—Coblenz—Trier— Diedenhofen—Montmédy—Charleville—Vouziers and detrained at Savigny on the 15th, coming into line south-west of Laon before the end of the month. It held this sector during a quiet period and was relieved by the 75th Reserve Division at the end of December after a month of rest. The 6th Division returned to relieve the 6th Bavarian Reserve Division in the sector to the right of the previous one, which it held until it was relieved by the 6th Bavarian Reserve Division on the 25th February.

General.

The 6th Division has a great reputation: it has always been considered one of the crack German divisions. Its fighting value, however, has naturally suffered as a result of its heavy losses before Verdun. Practically the whole of its fine officers' corps have been killed or disabled, and the reserve officers, who have filled the gaps, do not possess the confidence of their men. The division is composed almost entirely of Brandenburger, who are well-known for their dash and vigour. The division, however, has had some heavy fighting during 1917 and its *moral* may have suffered somewhat in the process.

The 6th Division is commanded by Lieut.-Gen. Herhudt von Rohden.

NOTE ON THE 7th DIVISION.

Composition.

The 7th Division is recruited in the IV. Army Corps District (Prussian Saxony). It originally consisted of the 13th Infantry Brigade (26th and 66th Infantry Regiments) and the 14th Infantry Brigade (27th and 165th Infantry Regiments). In March, 1915, the 66th Infantry Regiment was withdrawn to form part of the reconstituted 52nd Division, and the remaining three infantry regiments were grouped together in the 14th Infantry Brigade. In September, 1916, the 27th Infantry Regiment was withdrawn to join a new 211th Division. Its place in the 7th Division was taken by a newly-formed 393rd Infantry Regiment. This regiment was formed by grouping together elements withdrawn from regiments of the 7th, 8th, and 12th Divisions, the 50th Reserve Division and the 38th Landwehr Brigade.

History, 1914.

On mobilization, the IV. Corps (7th and 8th Divisions) was incorporated in the First German Army under von Kluck. It took part in the siege of Louvain, the entry into Brussels, the battle of Mons, and the battle of the Marne. In September, 1914, during the battle of the Aisne, it was engaged against the British left wing east of Soissons. Towards the end of the month, it was transferred from the First Army to the Sixth Army under the Crown Prince of Bavaria. In the early days of October, after attacking south of Arras, the Corps established its line from south of the Scarpe to Monchy-au-Bois.

1915.

In the first fortnight of June, 1915, the 7th Division was relieved south of the Scarpe by the I. Bavarian Reserve Corps, and both divisions of the IV. Corps came up to relieve the 117th Division, which had had to bear the brunt of the French attacks at Notre Dame de Lorette and Souchez. Elements of the 7th Division took part in the counter-attacks which followed the British offensive at Loos in September, 1915. The division, with the 8th Division, remained in the Loos—Lens sector until the battle of the Somme.

1916.

On the 3rd July, 1916, the IV. Corps was replaced on the Loos—Lens front by the extension southwards of the II. Bavarian Corps and the 5th Bavarian Division, and marched *via* Flines and Douai to Flers, where it arrived on the morning of the 16th July. The Corps was thrown into the battle immediately on the Pozières—Longueval—Delville Wood front, and suffered extraordinarily heavy losses in its fruitless attempts to recover the ground lost by the divisions previously in line. On the 28th July, the Corps was relieved by the IX. Reserve Corps and went to refit in the Valenciennes area. Thence it went into line in a quiet sector opposite Arras. After five weeks' rest, the Corps was again called upon to take part in the Somme battle. It was relieved opposite Arras by the IX. Corps and came into line in the Thiepval—Courcelette sector, where it replaced the 45th Reserve Division on about the 18th September. Here again it saw very heavy fighting and suffered severely. It was relieved on the 1st October—the 7th Division by the 2nd Naval Division—and returned to its old sector on the Loos salient. The 7th Division first relieved the 53rd Reserve Division south-east of Loos, but on the 10th November was relieved and transferred to the sector south of the La Bassée Canal, where it took up its position on the right flank of the 8th Division.

The total casualties admitted officially for two of the regiments of the 7th Division for their two visits to the Somme are as follows:—

	Total casualties.		Percentage of Establishment.
26th Inf. Regt. ...	...	3,625	...	121
165th Inf. Regt. ...	...	3,328	...	111

The 7th Division was relieved south of the La Bassée Canal by the 185th Division on the 10th May and went into reserve in the Menin—Courtrai area, where a British offensive was expected by the German Higher Command. On the 8th June, the day following the British attack on the Wytschaete—Messines ridge, the division went into line north-east of Wytschaete and relieved the exhausted 35th Division. Although fighting on a large scale had practically ceased, when the division came into line, it suffered severely in attempting to stay the British advance. After only seven days in line it was replaced by the 24th Division. It entrained at Roubaix on the 18th June, and travelled *viâ* Lille—Valenciennes—Charleville—Sedan—Metz to Dieuze, in Lorraine. On the 3rd July it continued its journey and proceeded *viâ* Saarburg—Strassburg—Freiburg—to Mülhausen.

The 7th Division rested in Alsace till the end of July. It entrained on the 27th-28th July, and travelled *viâ* Mülhausen—Colmar—Strassburg—Saargemünd—Metz—Sedan—Charleville—Valenciennes to Blaton (north of Condé-sur-l'Escaut). On the 2nd-3rd August the division re-entrained and travelled *viâ* Tournai—Lille—to Carvin, relieving the 8th Division east of Loos about the 5th-6th August. The division lost very heavily in the Canadian attack on the 15th August. It was driven from Hill 70, and suffered heavy casualties in attempting to recapture the hill. The 26th and 165th Regiments lost about two-thirds of their strength.

After resting and refitting in the Carvin—Lille area, the 7th Division went into line on the 21st September south of the La Bassée Canal and relieved the 185th Division. On the 19th October, the division was replaced by the 6th Bavarian Division and marched to Bauvin, where it entrained for Flanders, travelling *viâ* Lille and Courtrai to Harlebeke. It came into line on about the 29th October in the Becelaere sector and relieved the 15th Division. On the 5th November, it went out into reserve on relief by the 15th Division, and returned to the front line again on the 13th November. After six days in line it was replaced by the 17th Reserve Division, with which unit it alternated in the Becelaere sector until the end of the year. Although the division was not engaged in any fighting on a large scale, its losses in this sector were probably fairly heavy from artillery fire and owing to the climatic conditions. Elements of the division took part in a successful counter-attack on Polderhoek Château on the 6th November.

General. The 7th Division is a good division. It has fought well and tenaciously in the many battles it has been engaged in. Its *moral* can be described as good.

The 7th Division is commanded by Maj.-Gen. von der Esch.

NOTE ON THE 8th DIVISION.

Composition. The 8th Division is recruited in the IV. Army Corps District (Prussian Saxony). The most important towns in the Army Corps District are Magdeburg, Halle a/S., Halberstadt, Torgau, Altenburg and Dessau.

The 8th Division originally consisted of the 15th and 16th Infantry Brigades, the 15th having the 36th Fusilier Regiment and the 93rd Infantry Regiment, and the 16th having the 72nd Infantry Regiment and 153rd Infantry Regiment.

In March, 1915, the 36th Fusilier Regiment was withdrawn to form part of the reconstituted 113th Division, and the remaining three infantry regiments were grouped together in the 16th Infantry Brigade.

History, 1914. On mobilization, the IV. Corps (7th and 8th Divisions) was incorporated with the First German Army under von Kluck. It took part in the siege of Louvain, the entry into Brussels, the battle of Mons, and the battle of the Marne. In September, 1914, it was engaged against the British left wing east of Soissons, during the battle of the Aisne. Towards the end of September, 1914, it was transferred from the First Army to the Sixth Army, under the Crown Prince of Bavaria. In the early days of October, 1914, after attacking south of Arras, the Corps

1915. established its line from south of the Scarpe to Monchy-au-Bois. At the end of May, 1915, the 8th Division was relieved in the Monchy sector by the 111th Division, and withdrawn into Army Reserve near Douai. In the first fortnight of June, the 7th Division was relieved south of the Scarpe by the I. Bavarian Reserve Corps, and both divisions of the IV. Corps came up to relieve the 117th Division, which had had to bear the brunt of the French attacks at Notre Dame de Lorette and Souchez.

After having resisted the French attacks at Souchez in May and June together with the 7th Division, the 8th Division was relieved at the beginning of September by the 123rd Division, and went into Army Reserve in the neighbourhood of Roubaix—Tourcoing. At the battle of Loos, the 8th Division was rushed up hurriedly to take part in the counter-attacks against Loos. Here it established itself in its new line and was later joined by the 7th Division.

1916. The IV. Army Corps was not seriously engaged in 1916 until the battle of the Somme. On the 3rd July, it was replaced on the Loos—Lens front by the extension southwards of the II. Bavarian Army Corps and the 5th Bavarian Division, and marched *viâ* Flines and Douai to Flers, where it arrived on the morning of the 16th July. The Corps was thrown into the battle immediately on the Pozières—Longueval—Delville Wood front, and suffered extraordinarily heavy losses in its fruitless attempts to recover the ground lost by the divisions previously in line on this front. On the 28th July, the Corps was relieved by the IX. Reserve Army Corps, and went to refit in the Valenciennes area. Thence it went into line in a quiet sector opposite Arras relieving the I. Bavarian Reserve Corps and the 38th Landwehr Brigade on the 9th August. After five weeks' rest on this front, the Corps was again called upon to take part in the Somme battle. It was relieved opposite Arras by the IX. Army Corps and came into line in the Thiepval—Courcelette sector, where it replaced the 45th Reserve Division on about the 18th September. Here again it saw very heavy fighting and suffered severely. It was relieved on the 1st October; the 7th Division by the 2nd Naval Division, and the 8th Division by the 4th Ersatz Division. It then returned to its old sector on the Loos salient, where the 7th Division relieved the 53rd Reserve Division south-east of Loos, while the 8th Division relieved the 54th Reserve Division north-east of Loos. The 7th Division, however, was relieved by the 11th Reserve Division on the 10th November, and came into line again almost immediately on the right flank of the 8th Division, where it replaced the 50th Reserve Division south of La Bassée Canal.

The total casualties, admitted officially, for the 8th Division for its two visits to the Somme are as follows :—

	Total Casualties.		Percentage of Establishment.
8th Division	7,878	...	87·5
153rd Inf. Regt. (8th Div.) ...	3,002	...	100
72nd Inf. Regt. (8th Div.) ...	2,556	...	85
93rd Inf. Regt. (8th Div.) ...	2,320	...	77

1917. During the winter of 1916-1917, the IV. Army Corps was not engaged in any fighting on a large scale. In April, May and June, however, heavy casualties were inflicted on the 8th Division in the course of numerous raids which were carried out against it by British troops. The 153rd Regiment alone lost 130 prisoners. At the end of July and early in August the 8th Division suffered severely from artillery fire, and when the British attack north of Lens became imminent was relieved by the 7th Division.

The 8th Division entrained on the 5th August in the Carvin area and detrained on the following day in the area west of Rethel.

It came into line in the Reims area on the 9th August, relieving the 51st Reserve Division south of Ripont. After five quiet weeks in this sector it was relieved by the 80th Reserve Division and sent to Flanders. Entraining at Semide, near Vouziers, on the 18th September, it travelled *viâ* Launois—Charleville—Mouzon—Givet—Dinant—Namur—Charleroi—Courcelles—Motte—Mons—Tournai, and detrained at Lauwe early on the following morning. From here, the division marched to Halluin and Menin. It came into line on the 30th, when it relieved the 19th Reserve Division west of Becelaere. The 8th Division was engaged in the British attacks of the 4th October, and is known to have suffered severely. It was relieved on the 6th by the 10th Bavarian Division, and was moved to a quieter sector, relieving the 24th Division three days later in the Houthem sector. The losses of the division during its week in the Becelaere sector were very heavy indeed. The 2nd Battalion of the 72nd Regiment came out of line only 80 strong, while the rifle strength of each regiment was reduced to 700 or below. While in the Houthem sector the 8th Division was not engaged in any fighting, and remained in line until the end of January, 1918. It **1918.** was then relieved by the 17th Reserve Division, and during February was at rest in the Courtrai area, where it underwent a course of training.

General. After the fighting in 1914 the 8th Division has confined itself almost entirely to the defensive. It has, however, always fought well when attacked and defended its position stubbornly. During the third battle of Ypres there was evidence of a deterioration in *moral*, but there is no reason for thinking that this was more than temporary.

The 8th Division is commanded by Major-General Hamann.

NOTE ON THE 11th DIVISION.

Composition. The 11th Division is recruited in the VI. Army Corps District, and has its headquarters at Breslau. The VI. Army Corps District comprises the towns of Breslau, Schweidnitz, Gleiwitz, Neisse, Glatz, Oppeln, Glogau, Leobschütz.

The 11th Division originally consisted of the 21st Infantry Brigade (10th Grenadier Regiment and 38th Fusilier Regiment) and 22nd Infantry Brigade (11th Grenadier Regiment and 51st Infantry Regiment). The 11th Grenadier Regiment was withdrawn in November, 1916, and transferred to Macedonia, where it was attached to the 101st Division. The remaining three infantry regiments, *i.e.*, 10th Grenadier Regiment, 38th Fusilier Regiment and 51st Infantry Regiment, were then grouped together in the 21st Infantry Brigade.

History, 1914. At the beginning of the war, the VI. Corps (11th and 12th Divisions) formed part of the Fifth Army under the Crown Prince, which took part in the battle of Longwy in August, 1914. When the German advance had reached its high water-mark on the 7th September, the VI. Corps was near Revigny, west of Bar-le-Duc.

After the battle of the Marne, the VI. Corps was transferred to the Third Army, and, on the 21st September, was fighting at Berru and Nogent l'Abbesse, just east of Reims. On the 4th October, 1914, the 11th Division was engaged at Binarville (Argonne), having left the 12th Division on the Reims front. By the 27th October, the 22nd Infantry Brigade (11th Division) had rejoined the 12th Division at Beine, east of Reims, and the VI. Corps (less the 21st Brigade detached in the Argonne) remained in front of Reims until the middle of June, 1915.

1915.

At the end of January, 1915, the 21st Brigade rejoined the VI. Corps in the Reims sector, but the 6th *Jäger* Battalion remained in the Argonne, attached to the XVI. Corps, and has never returned to the VI. Corps. In February, 1915, the 22nd Brigade was transferred temporarily to eastern Champagne to support the VIII. Reserve Corps.

About the middle of June, 1915, the whole of the VI. Corps was relieved by the XII. Corps on the Reims front and transferred to Artois, to reinforce the Sixth Army against the French offensive. By the end of June, the VI. Corps had taken over the front from north of Souchez to east of Neuville St. Vaast, where it relieved the VIII. Corps, which had suffered heavily.

At the end of September, 1915, the 11th Division was relieved in the sector south of Souchez by the 1st Guard Division, and the 12th Division, on its left, was relieved by von Hartz's Division.

The whole Corps was then moved south, and detrained in the Cambrai area, early in October, relieving the I. Bavarian Corps in the sector astride the Somme.

The VI. Gorps was engaged in heavy fighting in the Souchez-Neuville sector during the summer and autumn of 1915, but passed a quieter time after its arrival in the Somme area. At the end of January, 1916, the 11th Division carried out a local attack on the flank of the French Sixth Army, in which it succeeded in capturing the village of Frise on the left bank of the Somme, but suffered fairly heavy losses.

1916.

On the 25th May, the 11th Division was relieved by the 121st Division just south of the Somme, and shortly afterwards took over the sector of the 10th Bavarian Division south of the Amiens—St. Quentin road.

In this sector, the division bore the brunt of the French attack on the 1st July and following days. The 11th Division suffered extremely heavy losses, and left a large number of prisoners in the hands of the French. It was withdrawn towards the end of July, and brought to the Roye area, where it relieved the 2nd Guard Division about the 1st August.

After a month's rest in this quiet sector, the division was relieved by the 8th Bavarian Reserve Division, and brought back to the Somme for a second time. It took over the Berny—Vermandovillers sector and again saw extremely heavy fighting.

The total casualties admitted officially for the 11th Division for its two visits to the Somme were 9,912, or 83 per cent. of establishment.

The 11th Division was relieved south of the River Somme on the 10th October by the 44th Reserve Division, and was transferred *via* Rethel to Champagne, where it relieved the 22nd Reserve Division in the Prunay sector on the 24th October.

The 11th Division was replaced in the Prunay sector on the 12th December by the 12th Division, and came to rest in the St. Quentin area.

1917.

On the 4th January, it came into line in the Lassigny sector (Oise), where it relieved the 44th Reserve Division. This division returned to its old position on the 10th February, and the 11th Division was then brought to the Ablaincourt sector (south of River Somme), where it relieved the 21st Division.

About the middle of March, the 11th Division, with the German forces engaged on the Somme, withdrew to the Hindenburg line. On arrival in the St. Quentin area, the division was withdrawn and transferred *via* Etreux—Monceaux St. Vaast—Aniche—Douai and Roeux to the Arras front, where a British attack was believed to be imminent. Here it relieved the 24th Reserve Division in the sector just south of the River Scarpe on the 29th March.

On the 9th April, the 11th Division met the full shock of the British attack. Although showing a stubborn defence, the division was completely routed, and left over 2,200 prisoners in the hands of the British. It was relieved on the 11th April by the 3rd Bavarian Division, and transferred to the Bruges area to rest and refit. The division suffered very heavy losses during this fighting. The 51st Regiment came out with 600 men, the 12th Company being reduced to six men.

When, early in June, a British attack on the Wytschaete—Messines front became evident, the 11th Division was brought up as a reinforcement. On the 8th June, the day after the successful British assault, the division supported the 204th, 7th and 24th Divisions, which had been severely handled. It ultimately took over the sector east of Wytschaete, where it remained until it was relieved on the 26th June by the 18th Reserve Division.

The 11th Division rested in the area north of Lille for eight or nine days. It was then transferred by rail to Metz, and came into line in the Flirey sector, in Woëvre, where it relieved the Guard Ersatz Division. It remained in line in Woëvre until the end of August. It was then relieved by the 34th Division and went to rest near Metz for about a month. Early in October, the division moved to Champagne, and went into line in the Somme-Py sector, remaining there three or four weeks.

17

On the 2nd November, the division entrained at Semide, travelling *via* Valenciennes—Audenarde—Ingelmunster to Roulers, and relieving the 39th Division in the Passchendaele sector on the 5th November. On the following day it was engaged in the British attack, which resulted in the capture of Passchendaele. The division suffered both in the attack itself and in subsequent counter-attacks. On the 7th, the 11th Division was relieved by the 44th Reserve Division and went out to rest. The Flanders battle was now at an end, and the 11th Division was not called upon for further employment on that front. During December it was moved south into the Charleville area, and about the 18th February, 1918, relieved the 51st Reserve Division south-east of Tahure.

1918.

General.

The 11th Division is recruited from the prosperous mining and manufacturing district of Silesia. In spite of its heavy losses on the Somme, at Arras and at Wytschaete, it has always fought well. Its *moral* is affected by a certain admixture of Poles, who are generally ready to desert when opportunity offers.

The 11th Division is commanded by Major-Gen. von Etzel.

NOTE ON THE 12th DIVISION.

Composition.

The 12th Division is recruited in the VI. Army Corps District, and has its headquarters at Breslau. The VI. Army Corps District comprises the towns of Breslau, Schweidnitz, Gleiwitz, Neisse, Glatz, Oppeln, Glogau and Leobschütz.

The 12th Division originally consisted of the 24th Infantry Brigade (23rd and 62nd Infantry Regiments) and 78th Infantry Brigade (63rd and 157th Infantry Regiments). The 157th Infantry Regiment was withdrawn to join a new 117th Division in April, 1915, and the remaining three regiments of the division were grouped in the 24th Infantry Brigade.

History, 1914.

At the beginning of the war, the VI. Corps (11th and 12th Divisions) formed part of the Fifth Army under the Crown Prince, which took part in the battle of Longwy in August, 1914. When the German advance had reached its high watermark on the 7th September, the VI. Corps was near Revigny, west of Bar-le-Duc.

After the battle of the Marne, the VI. Corps was transferred to the Third Army, and, on the 21st September, was fighting at Berru and Nogent l'Abbesse, just east of Reims. On the 4th October, 1914, the 11th Division was engaged at Binarville (Argonne), having left the 12th Division on the Reims front. By the 27th October, the 22nd Infantry Brigade (11th Division) had rejoined the 12th Division at Beine, east of Reims, and the VI. Corps (less the 21st Brigade detached in the Argonne) remained in front of Reims until the middle of June, 1915.

1915.

At the end of January, 1915, the 21st Brigade rejoined the VI. Corps in the Reims sector, but the 6th *Jäger* Battalion remained in the Argonne, attached to the XVI. Corps, and has never returned to the VI. Corps. In February, 1915, the 22nd Brigade was transferred temporarily to eastern Champagne to support the VIII. Reserve Corps.

About the middle of June, 1915, the whole of the VI. Corps was relieved by the XII. Corps on the Reims front and transferred to Artois, to reinforce the Sixth Army against the French offensive. By the end of June, the VI. Corps had taken over the front from north of Souchez to east of Neuville St. Vaast, where it relieved the VIII Corps, which had suffered heavily.

At the end of September, 1915, the 11th Division was relieved in the sector south of Souchez by the 1st Guard Division, and the 12th Division, on its left, was relieved by von Hartz's Division.

The whole Corps was then moved south, and detrained in the Cambrai area early in October, relieving the I. Bavarian Corps in the sector astride the Somme.

The VI. Corps was engaged in heavy fighting in the Souchez—Neuville sector during the summer and autumn of 1915, but passed a quiet time after its arrival in the Somme area in November. The VI. Corps with both its divisions remained in this area until the beginning of the Somme battle.

1916.

On the 1st July, the 12th Division met the full weight of the British attack north of the River Somme, in the Contalmaison-Hardecourt sector, and suffered extremely heavy losses in its efforts to hold up the British advance. It was withdrawn on about the 12th July to refit at Cambrai.

The total casualties, admitted officially, for the fighting between the 1st and 12th July, were 5,535, or 61·5 per cent. of establishment.

On about the 20th July, the 12th Division was again called upon to take part in the Somme battle. It came into line in the sector north-east of Pozières, and was severly handled in the ensuing fighting. It was withdrawn from this sector on about the 9th August, and on the 21st August relieved the 111th Division in the quiet sector between Monchy-au-Bois and Blaireville (south of Arras). The 12th Division held this sector till the 10th October, when it was relieved by the 26th Reserve Division.

The 12th Division next came into action on the 25th-26th October in the sector north of the River Ancre, relieving elements of the 2nd Guard Reserve Division. On the 14th November, British troops took the offensive north of the Ancre area, captured Beaumont-Hamel and Beaucourt, and inflicted serious losses on the 12th Division.

The division was relieved on the 19th November by the 208th Division, and was transferred to Champagne, where it relieved the 11th Division in the sector north-east of Prunay on the 12th December.

Towards the end of December, the 12th Division was withdrawn from this quiet sector, and replaced by the 14th Reserve Division. It entrained on the 28th December at Warmériville (north-east of Reims), and travelled to Russia *via* Aachen—Cologne—Hanover—Lüneburg—Hamburg— Stettin — Königsberg—Tilsit—Shavli—Ponieviej, detraining south-west of Illutsk on the 2nd January. It began relieving the 2nd Division in the sector in front of Dvinsk on the same day. During the five months the division spent on the Russian front it was not engaged in any infantry fighting worth mentioning. It was relieved towards the end of May by the 232nd Division, and returned to the Western front. It entrained at Elovka, near Dvinsk, on the 27th May, and travelled *via* Insterburg—Schneidemühl—Posen—Frankfurt a/O.—Leipzig—Gera—Weimar—Cologne—Saarbrücken, detraining at Metz on the 3rd June. It re-entrained on the 9th June at Ars-sur-Moselle and continued its journey *via* Metz—Luxemburg—Namur—Ath—Tournai to Mouscron, whence it marched to Gheluwe.

The 12th Division was probably intended as a reinforcement for the Wytschaete—Messines front, but, as the British attacks in this area were not continued after the original objectives had been gained, it was not required and remained in reserve. When, however, towards the end of July, a British attack on a large scale from the direction of Ypres became imminent, the division was sent up to this front, and, on the 1st August, the day following the successful Franco-British attack, it relieved the 22nd Reserve Division in the sector east of Klein Zillebeke. In this sector, the division was not engaged to any extent in infantry fighting, but suffered severely from shell fire. It was relieved on the 20th August by the 9th Reserve Division, and was transferred to Alsace to rest and refit. The 62nd Infantry Regiment suffered very heavy losses in Flanders, the 3rd Battalion suffering in particular. The 12th Division remained near the Swiss frontier throughout August and September, during which time it was equipped as a mountain division in view of the approaching German campaign in Italy. Towards the end of September, the division left Alsace, and detrained at Klagenfurt, whence it marched to Grahovo, near Tolmino. On the 25th October it was engaged in the capture of Monte Matajour (south-west of Caporetto), and a week later the German communiqués made mention of 12th Division troops in connection with the fighting on the Tagliamento. It held a sector on the lower course of the river, and was grouped under the III. Bavarian Corps. Early in December, it was identified by contact on the Piave, but was relieved on the 8th by the 35th Austrian Division and left the Italian front, arriving in the Freiburg area towards the end of the month. During January, 1918, the 12th Division remained in the neighbourhood of Zabern, and on the 5th February relieved the 233rd Division in the Domèvre area (Lorraine).

Uniform. In recognition of its services in Italy in 1917, the Emperor of Austria is now Colonel-in-Chief of the 63rd Infantry Regiment, which now wears the Emperor Karl's cipher on the shoulder-straps instead of the number 63.

Prisoners captured during 1917 state that the regiments of the 12th Division are distinguished by small pieces of coloured ribbon tied round their shoulder-straps. The colours are as follows :—

23rd Infantry Regiment	...	...	...	Red.
62nd Infantry Regiment	...	...	...	Blue.
63rd Infantry Regiment	...	...	...	Yellow.

General. The 12th Division is recruited from the prosperous mining and manufacturing district of Silesia. It acquitted itself well in the fighting on the Somme in 1916. At Ypres, in 1917, too few prisoners of this division were captured to be able to gauge the state of the *moral* with any accuracy. Its *moral* is affected by a certain admixture of Poles, who are generally ready to desert when opportunity offers.

The 12th Division is commanded by Lieut.-General Lequis.

NOTE ON THE 13th DIVISION.

The 13th and 14th Divisions together form the VII. Army Corps, and both divisions are recruited in the VII. Army Corps District, which includes Westphalia, with the towns of Dortmund, Bochum, Duisburg, Elberfeld, Düsseldorf, Münster and Cologne.

Composition. The 13th Division originally consisted of the 25th Infantry Brigade (13th and 158th Infantry Regiments) and the 26th Infantry Brigade (15th and 55th Infantry Regiments). In March, 1915, the 158th Infantry Regiment was withdrawn to join the 50th Reconstituted Division, and the three remaining regiments were grouped in the 26th Infantry Brigade.

History, 1914. At the beginning of the war the VII. Corps formed part of the Second Army under von Bülow, and advanced into France *via* Namur. When the great outflanking movement began, the VII. Corps was transferred to the Seventh Army and remained in position north of Reims. During October, 1914, the corps moved north and became part of the Sixth Army under Prince Rupprecht of Bavaria. From October, 1914, to March, 1916, the corps held almost the same sector, *i.e.*, from east of Fauquissart to east of Cambrin.

1917.
1918.

1915.   The VII. Corps was strongly attacked by the British in 1915, at Neuve Chapelle in March and at Festubert in June. On both occasions the German line was broken and the corps displayed considerable defensive tenacity. At the same time, losses were heavy. In September elements of the corps were sent to support the 117th Division near Loos, and again suffered severe casualties. During the period spent by the corps in this area a great deal of mining work was carried out between Givenchy and south of the Béthune—La Bassée road.

1916.   At the end of March, 1916, the VII. Corps was relieved by the XXVII. Reserve Corps and withdrawn to rest in the Tournai area. At the beginning of June the VII. Corps was transferred to the Verdun front *via* Hirson and Charleville, and was engaged on the left bank of the Meuse. The 13th Division relieved the 22nd Reserve Division west of Cumières. It remained in this sector until September, during which time it was fairly continuously engaged in sharp fighting, and sustained appreciable losses. On the 7th September the 13th Division entrained at Vilosnes-sur-Meuse, and, moving *via* Sedan—Charleville—Hirson—Cambrai, detrained at Roisel. It came into line on the 9th east of Clery, relieving elements of the 53rd Reserve Division. The division was engaged in heavy fighting and was relieved after a week by elements of the 25th and 212th Divisions. During this week it lost about 400 prisoners, and the total losses are estimated at about one-third of the effective strength of the division. The 13th Division returned at once to its old sector at Verdun and relieved the 38th Division in the Mort Homme region on the 28th September. It passed the winter and following spring in this sector and was relieved

1917.   in the middle of May by the 10th Reserve Division, whereupon it was brought up to the Aisne region and, after spending a few weeks near Laon, the 13th Division relieved the 11th Bavarian Division in the Cerny sector on the 10th June. It was engaged in fairly continuous fighting in this area throughout July, and on the 21st carried out an unsuccessful attack, supported by special assaulting troops. Early in August, the 13th Division was relieved by the 50th Division and moved to the St. Quentin region, where it replaced the 103rd Division south of La Fère on the 10th. After spending two uneventful months in this sector, it was relieved by the 10th Division, and returned to the Laon area, where it relieved the 103rd Division east of Laffaux Windmill. This relief took place shortly before the big French attack of the 23rd October. The 13th Division bore the whole brunt of this attack and suffered enormous losses. 1,850 prisoners were taken, including two regimental commanders and their staffs. The division was so shattered that it had to be withdrawn on the following day and did not reappear in line until the 18th December, when it relieved the 19th Reserve Division at Avocourt Wood on the west bank of

1918.   the Meuse. At the end of January, 1918, the 13th Division was relieved by the 13th Reserve Division and was withdrawn to the Arlon area.

General.   The 13th Division is a division of good quality. During 1915, the Westphalians distinguished themselves by excellent work on defences and fought tenaciously on all occasions. At Verdun and on the Somme, too, the division acquitted itself well. Both in 1916 and 1917, however, desertions were not infrequent, these being mostly on the part of Poles and Alsatians, who are found in fairly large numbers in the division. The division received a smashing blow on the Ailette in October, 1917, and the drafts required to bring it up to strength again have not yet been put to the test. It is therefore not possible to estimate the value of the division at the present moment.

    The 13th Division is commanded by Lieut.-General von Borries.

NOTE ON THE 14th DIVISION.

Composition.   The 13th and 14th Divisions together make up the VII. Army Corps, and both divisions are recruited from the VII. Army Corps District. This district, which comprises the province of Westphalia, includes the towns of Dortmund, Bochum, Duisburg, Elberfeld, Düsseldorf, Münster and Cologne.

    At the outbreak of war the 14th Division consisted of the 27th Infantry Brigade (16th and 53rd Infantry Regiments) and the 79th Infantry Brigade (56th and 57th Infantry Regiments). In March, 1915, the 53rd Infantry Regiment was withdrawn to join the reconstituted 50th Division, the three remaining regiments being grouped in the 79th Infantry Brigade.

**History,
1914.**   At the beginning of the war the VII. Corps formed part of the Second Army under von Bülow, and advanced into France *via* Namur. When the great outflanking movement began the VII. Corps was transferred to the Seventh Army and remained in position north of Reims. During October, 1914, the corps moved north and became part of the Sixth Army under Prince Rupprecht of Bavaria. From October, 1914, to March, 1916, the Corps held about the same sector, *i.e.*, from east of Fauquissart to east of Cambrin.

1915.   The VII. Corps was strongly attacked by the British in 1915—at Neuve Chapelle in March and at Festubert in May. On both occasions the German line was broken, and the corps displayed considerable defensive tenacity. At the same time, its losses were heavy, the 57th Infantry Regiment being reduced to the strength of three companies. In September elements of the corps were sent to support the 117th Division near Loos and again suffered severe casualties.

During the period spent by the corps in this area a great deal of mining work was carried out between Givenchy and south of the Béthune—La Bassée road. This was largely the work of the Westphalian miners of the 56th and 57th Infantry Regiments.

1916. At the end of March, 1916, the VII. Corps was relieved by the XXVII. Reserve Corps and withdrawn to rest in the Tournai area. At the beginning of June the corps was transferred to the Verdun front *via* Hirson and Charleville, and was engaged on the left bank of the Meuse. At the beginning of August the 14th Division was relieved on the left bank by the 1st Division and came into line on the right bank. Here it was engaged in much heavier fighting near the Thiaumont work and at Fleury, and its losses during August were heavy, although it fought well and with some success. At the end of the month the division was relieved by the 34th Division and returned to its former sector on the left bank. Not for long, however, for at the end of October it was back again on the right bank, and throughout November and December was engaged in fighting around Fort Douaumont. At the end of 1916 the 14th Division was withdrawn for a period of rest near Montmédy, and on the 27th January, 1917,

1917. returned to the Mort Homme sector, until the French offensive on the Aisne and in Champagne in the spring called for reinforcements in those sectors. The 14th Division entrained at Sivry-sur-Meuse on the 24th April and, moving *via* Sedan and Liart, detrained at Montcornet. It appeared in line on the 6th May and relieved the 1st Guard Division on the next day in the Hurtebise sector. After a week in line, during which it was engaged in continuous fighting on the Vauclerc Plateau, it was relieved by the 1st Bavarian Division and a week later elements appeared in line in the Craonne area, in support of the 11th Bavarian Division. The remainder of the division went to rest for three weeks at Oisy and then returned into line in the Hurtebise sector on the 21st June. It was again severely engaged, and on the 25th took part in heavy fighting round the Hurtebise Monument. The 57th Regiment suffered especially heavy losses, and the division as a whole had a very large number of casualties. The fighting died down considerably during July and the 14th Division remained in line until the 1st August, when it was withdrawn to rest at Vervins. In the middle of September it reappeared in the Laffaux area, south of the Ailette, and was still in line at the time of the big French attack in this area on the 23rd October. The 14th Division bore the full brunt of this attack and suffered enormous casualties. More than 1,750 prisoners were captured from the division, which had to be withdrawn on the following day, being relieved by the 6th Bavarian Reserve Division. On the 2nd November the 14th Division entrained in the Vervins area and travelled *via* Sedan and Conflans to Jaulny, and on about the 8th relieved the 195th Division in the Flirey sector (Woëvre). Previous to this, large drafts were sent from Germany and also from divisions on the Russian front to make good the losses on the Aisne, but, even so, the 43rd Field Artillery Regiment was too reduced in strength to be able to relieve the artillery of the 195th Division. The 14th Division spent the next two months quite uneventfully, but a smart raid by the French on the 8th January, 1918,

1918. resulted in the capture of 175 prisoners from the 14th Division. The division was relieved by the 78th Reserve Division on the night of the 13th-14th January and went to rest in the Metz area.

General. The 14th Division is one of good quality. All through the early stages of the war it distinguished itself by excellent work on defences, while fighting tenaciously on all occasions when it was attacked. It continued to fight well during its long engagement on the Verdun front, although losses during this period were heavy. During 1917, too, the division has had to face some very heavy fighting, and in October on the Aisne received a shattering blow at the hands of the French. Its present value is hard to estimate, as the quality of the more recent drafts has not been thoroughly tested.

The 14th Division is commanded by Major-General von Kraewel.

NOTE ON THE 15th DIVISION.

Composition. The 15th Division is recruited in the VIII. Army Corps District, and has its headquarters at Cologne. The VIII. Army Corps District comprises the towns of Cologne, Aachen, Bonn, Coblenz, Trier.

The 15th Division originally consisted of the 29th Infantry Brigade (25th and 161st Infantry Regiments) and the 80th Infantry Brigade (65th and 160th Infantry Regiments). During the summer and autumn of 1916, the infantry of the 15th Division was completely reorganized. The 29th Infantry Brigade was broken up—the 25th Infantry Regiment joining a new 208th Division, and the 161st Infantry Regiment going to the reconstituted 185th Division. The 65th Infantry Regiment was detached from the 80th Infantry Brigade and also joined the reconstituted 185th Division, leaving the 160th Infantry Regiment as the only original infantry unit still with the division. The three withdrawn regiments were replaced by only two regiments—the 186th Infantry Regiment (from the 185th Division) and a newly-formed 389th Infantry Regiment—which were grouped together with the 160th Infantry Regiment in the 80th Infantry Brigade. The 186th Infantry Regiment only fought with the 15th Division during September and October, 1916, and was then replaced by the 69th Infantry Regiment (from the 16th Division).

History,
1914.

In August, 1914, the VIII. Army Corps (15th and 16th Divisions) formed part of the Fourth German Army under Duke Albrecht of Württemberg. It marched into France by way of Luxemburg, and was not brought to a standstill until it had crossed the Marne in the Vitry-le-François area. Here the Corps suffered a severe defeat at the hands of the French, and retired in a northerly direction until it had reached the Hurlus—Perthes area in Champagne. In October, when the German Armies were regrouped, the VIII. Corps came under the orders of the Third German Army (von Einem).

1915.

Towards the end of December, 1914, the 15th Division was split up. The 29th Infantry Brigade was transferred from Champagne to Alsace, where it saw hard fighting in the Hartmannsweilerkopf area from January to April, 1915. The 80th Infantry Brigade remained in the Souain area (Champagne) until the beginning of April, and was then transferred to the Woëvre, where it was engaged in the Bois d'Ailly. About the middle of May, the 29th Infantry Brigade, which had been resting in the Briey area for three weeks, was joined by the 80th Infantry Brigade. The 15th Division was then transported to the area north of Arras to assist in repelling the French attacks in the Souchez—Neuville-Vitasse area. After suffering heavy losses, especially in the fighting about the Labyrinth, the division was transferred to the Aisne front, where it took over a quiet sector in the Soissons area.

1916.

The 15th Division remained in this sector, and was not seriously engaged until July, 1916. On the opening of the battle of the Somme, elements of the division were sent to form part of Liebert's composite division, which was engaged in the La Maisonette sector (south of the River Somme) on the 11th July and subsequent days. This division suffered very serious losses. On the 26th September, the bulk of the 15th Division (160th, 186th and 369th Infantry Regiments) arrived at Bohain from the Aisne to take part in the battle of the Somme. It came into line in the Rancourt sector (north of River Somme) on the 28th-29th September, and relieved the 213th and 214th Divisions. Hard fighting, in which the division was severely handled by the French, ensued. The 186th Infantry Regiment alone lost over 250 prisoners. The division was relieved on the 13th October by the 1st Bavarian Division and withdrawn to rest.

Towards the end of October, the 15th Division came into line in the Soissons sector, relieving the 213th Division. It only remained in line for about 10 days before it was withdrawn again and dispatched to the Russian front. The division (69th, 160th and 389th Infantry Regiments) was relieved by the 9th Division on the 10th November. It entrained about the middle of November in the Laon area, and travelled to the Russian front viâ Liége—Aachen—Düsseldorf—Hannover—Magdeburg—Berlin—Scernevitsi—Warsaw—Brest-Litovsk—Kovel, detraining at Turisk after a five days' journey (20th November). It went into line in the Kiselin sector, south of Kovel,

1917.

where it remained till the end of April, 1917, when it was again transferred to France. During its stay in Russia the division had a very quiet time, and suffered practically no casualties. On the 24th April, the 15th Division entrained at Rogitzno (Kovel area), and travelled viâ Kovel—Brest-Litovsk—Warsaw—Kalisch—Lissa—Kottbus—Leipzig—Erfurt—Bebra—Frankfurt a/M.—Kreuznach — Saarbrücken—Metz—Conflans, detraining at Vigneulles on the 29th April. The division was put into line in the Woëvre immediately to release the 10th Division for operations elsewhere, and after spending a month in this quiet sector was replaced by the 44th Reserve Division and transferred to the Aisne front.

The 15th Division came into line on the Vauclerc Plateau (Chemin des Dames) on the 30th May, and took the place of the 2nd Bavarian Division. In this sector it was engaged in fighting of the severest kind, and had very heavy casualties. Towards the beginning of July, after nearly five weeks in a battle sector, the 15th Division was relieved by the 5th Guard Division and transferred to Lorraine, where it came into line in the Blamont area on the 12th July and relieved the 219th Division.

During September, the 15th Division left Lorraine and came to the Verdun front. It did not, however, come into line in that area, but was transferred to Flanders on the 5th October, travelling viâ Longuyon—Charleville—Brussels—Ghent—Courtrai, and after a short rest, relieved the 10th Bavarian Division on the 13th October in the Becelaere sector (east of Ypres). Between October 13th and 31st, the 15th Division was in line for two periods of six days, alternating with the 10th Bavarian Division. For the first half of November, the 15th Division continued this same procedure, except that the 7th Division took the place of the 10th Bavarian Division. On the 13th November, the 15th Division was taken out for a month's rest in the Bruges—Knocke area. On its return to the front line, it came in to the Passchendaele sector, relieving the 16th Division on the 14th December. From this date until the 8th January, the 15th Division alternated with the 16th Division in holding the sector, the period in line for each division being six days. Altogether, in its two sectors, the division did five turns of duty in the line. On its withdrawal on the 9th January, the division went to rest and training in the Bruges area.

General.

The 15th Division has seen a great deal of fighting and has usually acquitted itself well. Prior to its arrival in Flanders it had not been engaged against the British. It contains good material, and is a fair average German division.

The 15th Division is commanded by Maj.-Gen. Tappen, who, prior to taking this command, had the reputation of being a very able Staff Officer.

NOTE ON THE 16th DIVISION.

Composition. The 16th Division is recruited in the VIII. Army Corps District and has its head-quarters at Trier. The VIII. Army Corps District comprises the towns of Cologne, Aachen, Bonn, Coblenz, Trier.

The 16th Division originally consisted of the 30th Infantry Brigade (28th and 68th Infantry Regiments) and the 31st Infantry Brigade (29th and 69th Infantry Regiments). The 69th Infantry Regiment was withdrawn during October, 1916, and the remaining three infantry regiments were grouped together in the 30th Infantry Brigade.

History, 1914. In August, 1914, the VIII. Army Corps (15th and 16th Divisions) formed part of the Fourth German Army under Duke Albrecht of Württemberg. It marched into France by way of Luxemburg and was not brought to a standstill until it had crossed the Marne in the Vitry-le-François area. Here the corps suffered a severe defeat at the hands of the French, and retired in a northerly direction until it had reached the Hurlus—Perthes area in Champagne. In October, when the German Armies were regrouped, the VIII. Corps came under the orders of the Third German Army (von Einem).

1915. During the winter of 1914-15 the 16th Division saw heavy fighting in the Souain—Perthes area, where it remained till it was withdrawn early in April to rest in the Briey area, north-west of Metz. About the middle of May it was transferred to the area north of Arras to assist in repelling the French attacks in the Souchez—Neuville-Vitasse sector. After suffering heavy losses the division was withdrawn and sent into line in a quiet sector on the Aisne, east of Soissons. At the end of October the 16th Division took over the Nouvron sector, west of Soissons.

1916. The 16th Division remained in this sector until it was relieved, at the end of July, by Dumrath's Composite Division. It entrained at Folembray on the 28th July, detrained at Ham and was brought by motors to Nesle. On the 30th July it relieved the 36th Division in the Maucourt sector, north-west of Roye. After only a week in line in this sector it was relieved by the 2nd Guard Division and transferred by Ham—St. Quentin—Busigny—Cambrai to Fremicourt. On the 9th-10th August, the 16th Division made its first appearance on the Somme, when it came into line in the Pozières—Thiepval sector, and relieved the 117th Division. Fighting of the severest kind took place here and the division suffered heavily at the hands of the British troops. After two weeks in line, it was replaced by the 4th Guard Division and sent to a quiet sector west of Berry-au-Bac, where it relieved the 23rd Division.

Early in October, the division was again called upon to take part in the Somme battle. It was relieved west of Berry-au-Bac on the 1st October by the 9th Bavarian Reserve Division, entrained at Laon and travelled *via* St. Quentin and Bohain to Bertry. It remained here till the 9th October, when it came into line in the Lesbœufs—Sailly-Saillisel sector, and relieved the 17th Reserve Division. In the heavy fighting which followed its entry into line the division suffered severely and left about 150 prisoners in the hands of the French. Again, after only a fortnight in line, the division had to be withdrawn and its place was taken by the 30th Division.

The 16th Division next appeared in line north of Soissons. It relieved the 185th Division on the 5th November, but was again withdrawn on the 16th November to be sent to the Russian front. The 211th Division took over the sector vacated by it. The division entrained about the middle of November in the Laon area, and travelled to the Russian front *via* Liége — Aachen — Düsseldorf — Hannover — Magdeburg — Berlin—Scernevitsi—Warsaw—Brest-Litovsk—Kovel, detraining at Turisk after a five days' journey (25th November). It went into line in the Kiselin sector, south of Kovel, where it remained till the beginning of May, 1917, when it was again trans-**1917.** ferred to France. During its stay in Russia the division had a very quiet time and suffered practically no casualties. The 16th Division entrained near Kiselin (Galicia) on the 17th May and travelled to France *via* Vladimir-Volinski—Kovel—Brest-Litovsk —Warsaw—Kalisch—Cottbus—Leipzig—Cassel—Giessen—Coblenz—Ahrweiler—Gerolstein—Sedan—Attigny (east of Rethel), where it detrained at 12.30 p.m. on the 21st May after a journey of 106½ hours, going into rest-billets at Ecordal. On the 4th June the division marched from Ecordal through Tourteron and Brieulles-sur-Bac to Beaumont. This march took two days; there were many cases of heat-stroke, some of which were fatal. On the 9th June, the division entrained at Mouzon (south-east of Sedan) and detrained at Lille on the 10th, having travelled *via* Sedan—Charleville—Hirson—Valenciennes and Orchies. The division marched to Wambrechies, where it rested until the 24th June. It then marched to Wervicq, and went into line at Warneton on the night of the 25th-26th, relieving the 207th Division.

The division was not engaged in this sector until the 31st July, when the British attacked on the front between Boesinghe and the river Lys. This successful attack was not pressed in the Warneton area, so that, although prisoners of all three regiments were captured and a certain amount of ground was lost, the division did not suffer heavy casualties. It was relieved by the 32nd Division at the beginning of September, and went to rest in the area east of Bruges. Early in October the 16th Division was transferred to the Ypres front. Elements were sent forward to support east of Zonnebeke on the 3rd October in view of an expected British attack. On the next day, these elements were severely engaged in our successful attack and were withdrawn. On the 6th October, the whole division came into line south-east of Poelcappelle and relieved the 187th Division. It was engaged in the local British attacks made on the 9th and 12th October and lost about 100 prisoners. It was replaced by the 5th Bavarian Reserve Division on the 12th October and was withdrawn to rest.

The 16th Division returned to the Ypres front on the 24th November, relieving the 36th Reserve Division north of Becelaere. After holding this sector for six days, it was replaced by the 36th Reserve Division, and, after six days spent in reserve, took over the sector east of Passchendaele from the 25th Division. It then alternated in this sector with the 15th Division, doing seven days in line and six days in reserve until it was relieved about the middle of January by the 25th Division.

1918.

General.

The 16th Division is a good fighting formation. Previous to its appearance on the Somme in 1916, the division had made a great reputation for itself and was known as " The Iron Division " (Die Eiserne Division). In the fighting on the Somme, however, it did not distinguish itself in any way. At Warneton and Ypres in 1917, the division fought tenaciously in spite of its heavy losses.

The 16th Division is commanded by Lieut.-Gen. Frhr. von Lüttwitz.

NOTE ON THE 17th DIVISION.

Composition.

The 17th Division is recruited in the IX. Army Corps District (Schleswig-Holstein and Mecklenburg. The most important towns in the Corps district are Hamburg, Altona, Bremen, Lübeck and Rostock.

The 17th Division was at first composed of the 33rd Infantry Brigade (75th and 76th Infantry Regiments) and the 34th Infantry Brigade (89th Grenadier Regiment and 90th Fusilier Regiment). In April, 1915, the 76th Infantry Regiment was withdrawn to join the new 111th Division, and the three remaining regiments of the 17th Division were grouped in the 34th Infantry Brigade.

History, 1914.

1915.

1916.

In August, 1914, the IX. Army Corps (17th and 18th Divisions) formed part of the First German Army under von Kluck. It took part in the battle of Mons, the march on Paris, the battle of the Marne and the retreat to the Aisne. On the 13th September, on the commencement of trench warfare, the Corps took up its position between the Oise and Aisne, and remained there till the middle of November, 1915. Some of the resting battalions of the Corps were sent to the Champagne to reinforce the XII. Reserve Corps on the opening of the French offensive in September, 1915. The whole Corps was withdrawn from the Oise—Aisne sector at the end of November, and went into line north of Souain in Champagne, where it took part in the strong counter-attack delivered on this front. It remained in Champagne till the middle of June, 1916, and was then withdrawn to rest in the Charleville area.

In July, 1916, the 17th and 18th Divisions were brought to the Somme. The 17th Division entrained at Boulzicourt, Poixterron and Saulces-Monclin on the 2nd, 3rd and 4th of July, travelled *viâ* Charleville, Hirson and La Capelle, and detrained at and near St. Quentin. It came into line in the Barleux sector, just south of the Somme, on the 10th July, relieving the 22nd Reserve Division. The 18th Division entrained at Wasigny between the 2nd and 4th July, travelled *viâ* Laon and Tergnier and detrained at Ham. On the 12th July, it also was put into line in the Belloy—Berny sector on the left of the 17th Division. At the end of July, after some extremely heavy fighting, the IX. Corps was relieved by the Guard Reserve Corps and withdrawn to rest. The Corps was put into line again in the same sector on the 20th August, replacing the Guard Reserve Corps. During its second spell on the Somme, the Corps was again severely handled by the French, losing 950 prisoners between the 4th and 9th of August. The total casualties, admitted officially, for the 17th Division for its two visits to the Somme were 8,123, or 90 per cent. of its establishment.

The IX. Corps was relieved on the Somme about the middle of September by the 58th Division and 10th Ersatz Division, and transferred to the sector opposite Arras, where it relieved the IV. Corps. The Corps remained in this sector till December, when it was called upon to reinforce the Ancre front. The 18th Division was relieved on the 12th December by the 23rd Reserve Division, and went into line astride the Ancre 10 days later, replacing the 50th Reserve Division. The 17th Division, which was relieved opposite Arras by the 24th Reserve Division on the 24th December, followed the 18th Division to the Ancre front and came into line on its left, in the Pys sector, on the 11th January, relieving the 56th Division. In the fighting about Grandcourt and Miraumont, which took place during January and February, 1917, both divisions again suffered severely; the 17th Division lost 250 prisoners and the 18th Division 220 prisoners. About the 20th March, when the Germans shortened their front by retiring to the Hindenburg line, the IX. Corps was withdrawn to rest.

1917.

On the opening of the British offensive, astride the Scarpe, the IX. Corps was rushed up to reinforce the front north-east of Arras. The 17th Division relieved the 1st Bavarian Reserve Division on the Oppy—Gavrelle front on the 10th April, and suffered severely in the counter-attacks which it carried out. It was withdrawn on the 25th April, and its place was taken by the 1st Guard Reserve Division. The division rested in the Tournai area till about the 9th May, and then went into line in the Boursies—Demicourt sector (west of Cambrai), relieving the 38th Division. On the 28th May, it was replaced in this quiet sector by the 221st Division and withdrawn to the Cambrai area to rest.

After a comparatively short period of rest, the 17th Division was alarmed and transported to Flanders. It entrained on the 9th June at Cambrai and travelled *via* Valenciennes and Mons to Roulers. On the 13th June, it came into line north of Hooge (east of Ypres), and reinforced the front between the 119th and 233rd Divisions. Besides suffering heavy casualties from the preliminary bombardment to the imminent battle of Ypres, the division lost some 80 prisoners in raids. Owing to these losses, it was replaced by the 38th Division on the 27th July, three days before the British attack took place.

The 17th Division next appeared in line in a quiet sector south-west of Cambrai, where it had replaced the 121st Division about the middle of August. After some five weeks in this area, it was again found fit to take part in the battle of Ypres. The division was relieved by the 204th Division on the 23rd September, and travelled *via* Cambrai to Ledeghem, relieving the 50th Reserve Division in the Polygone Wood sector (north-east of Ypres) on the evening of the 26th September, where it suffered extremely heavy losses in fruitless counter-attacks carried out to recover the ground lost by the 50th Reserve Division on the morning of the 26th September. The 17th Division was relieved by the 19th Reserve Division on the 28th September, after only two days in line, and transferred to the area south of Lens, where it relieved the 36th Reserve Division on the 17th October. After four uneventful months in line on this front, the division was relieved by the 12th Reserve Division and went to rest.

General.
The 17th Division has seen a great deal of fighting and has usually acquitted itself well. The *moral* of the division in the battle of Ypres, however, was not good. The violence of the British artillery fire and the abnormal casualties suffered completely demoralized the men. Although there is no direct evidence, it can be assumed that the division lost at least 50 per cent. of its fighting strength in the two engagements at Ypres. The 17th Division includes a considerable number of Danes. These, however, fight well, and do not appear to be in any way a source of weakness.

The 17th Division is commanded by Lieut.-Gen. von Gabain.

NOTE ON THE 18th DIVISION.

Composition.
The 18th Division originally formed, with the 17th Division, the IX. Army Corps, which is recruited in Schleswig-Holstein and Mecklenburg. The most important towns in the Corps District are Hamburg, Altona, Bremen, Lübeck and Rostock, and the Headquarters are at Altona. The 18th Division originally consisted of the 35th Infantry Brigade (84th Infantry Regiment and 86th Fusilier Regiment), and the 36th Infantry Brigade (31st and 85th Infantry Regiments). In April, 1915, the 84th Infantry Regiment was withdrawn from the 18th Division to join the new 54th Division, the three remaining regiments being grouped in the 36th Infantry Brigade.

History, 1914.
In August, 1914, the IX. Army Corps formed part of the First German Army under von Kluck. It took part in the battle of Mons, the march on Paris, the battle of the Marne, and the retreat to the Aisne. On the 13th September, on the commencement of trench warfare, the Corps took up its position between the Oise

1915.
and Aisne and remained there till the middle of November, 1915. Some of the resting battalions of the Corps were sent to the Champagne to reinforce the XII. Reserve Corps on the opening of the French offensive in September, 1915. The whole Corps was withdrawn from the Oise—Aisne sector at the end of November, and went into line north of Souain in Champagne, where it took part in the strong counter-attack delivered on this front. It remained in Champagne till the middle

1916.
of June, 1916, when it was withdrawn to rest in the Charleville area.

In July, 1916, the 17th and 18th Divisions were brought to the Somme front. The 17th Division entrained at Boulzicourt, Poix-Terron and Saulces-Monclin on the 2nd, 3rd and 4th of July, travelled *via* Charleville—Hirson and La Capelle, and detrained at and near St. Quentin. It came into line in the Barleux sector, just south of the Somme, on the 10th July, relieving the 22nd Reserve Division. The 18th Division entrained at Wasigny between the 2nd and 4th July, travelled *via* Laon and Tergnier, and detrained at Ham. On the 12th July, it was also put into line in the Belloy—Berny sector on the left of the 17th Division. At the end of July, after some extremely heavy fighting, the IX. Corps was relieved by the Guard Reserve Corps, and withdrawn to rest. The Corps was put into line again in the same sector, on the 20th August, replacing the Guard Reserve Corps. During its second spell on the Somme, the Corps was again severely handled by the French, losing 950 prisoners between the 4th and 9th of August. The total casualties, admitted officially, for the 18th Division for its two visits to the Somme, were 8,444, or 94 per cent. of its establishment.

The IX. Corps was relieved on the Somme about the middle of September by the 58th Division and 10th Ersatz Division, and transferred to a sector opposite Arras, where it relieved the IV. Corps. The Corps remained in this sector till December, when it was called upon to reinforce the Ancre front. The 18th Division was relieved on the 12th December by the 23rd Reserve Division and went into line astride the Ancre 10 days later, replacing the 50th Reserve Division. The 17th Division, which was relieved opposite Arras by the 24th Reserve Division on the 24th December, followed the 18th Division to the Ancre front and came into line on its

1917. left, in the Pys sector, on the 11th January, relieving the 56th Division. In the fighting about Grandcourt and Miraumont, which took place during January and February, 1917, both divisions again suffered severely; the 17th Division lost 250 prisoners, and the 18th Division 220 prisoners. About the 20th March the IX. Corps was withdrawn to rest, the Germans having shortened their front by retiring to the Hindenburg line.

On the opening of the British offensive astride the Scarpe, the IX. Corps was rushed up to reinforce the front north-east of Arras. The 18th Division replaced the 14th Bavarian Division in the sector astride the Scarpe on the 11th April. In the fighting which ensued around Roeux it suffered such heavy losses that it had to be replaced by the 185th Division on the 22nd April. After a short period of rest, the division came into line in the Ribécourt sector (south-west of Cambrai) and relieved the 236th Division. About the 1st June, the division extended its front and took over the sector of the 17th Reserve Division on its right.

Towards the end of August, the 18th Division was replaced south-west of Cambrai by the 54th Division and transferred to Flanders. It entrained at Rieux, near Cambrai, on the 28th August, travelled *viâ* Valenciennes—Ghent to Beernem, and went to rest at Doomkerke (north of Thielt). On the 16th September it came from Beernem to Cortemarck and relieved the 26th Reserve Division in the Mangelaare sector. The division remained in line, a little over three weeks. It suffered considerably in the Franco-British advance of the 9th October, when the French took 244 unwounded prisoners of the division. The 18th Division was relieved immediately after this attack and was transferred to the Russian front. It entrained near Cortemarck about the 15th October and travelled *viâ* Lichtervelde—Thielt—Ghent—Louvain— Aachen—Bremen—Hamburg—Königsberg—Eydtkuhnen and arrived in the Vilna area on the 21st October. The division, however, only remained on the Russian front for a few weeks. It was withdrawn shortly before, and no doubt in anticipation of, the opening of negotiations for an armistice, and had arrived in the Mülhausen area by the end of November, having travelled *viâ* Vilna—Berlin—Nordhausen and Strassburg.

1918. The 18th Division rested in Alsace until the 12th February, when it entrained for the Cambrai area, where it relieved the 107th Division in the Gonnelieu area on the 15th February.

General. The 18th Division has had plenty of fighting experience. In the battle of Arras it was engaged in the defence of the village of Roeux. It fought there with tenacity and carried out its task creditably. In Flanders, the division failed, on certain occasions, to carry out counter-attacks as ordered, but this must be attributed rather to the extreme difficulty of the ground than to any general failure of *moral* in the division. The division has had a long rest, is no doubt up to strength and well trained, and should give a good account of itself. It includes a considerable number of Danes. These, however, fight well and do not appear to be in any way a source of weakness.

The 18th Division is commanded by Maj.-Gen. Frhr. von Massenbach.

NOTE ON THE 20th DIVISION.

Composition. The 20th Division, which with the 19th Division formed the X. Army Corps, is recruited in the Province of Hannover. The principal towns in this district are Hannover, Oldenburg, Braunschweig, Celle, Hildesheim, Osnabrück, Göttingen, Hameln, and Lüneburg.

Originally, the 20th Division consisted of the 39th Infantry Brigade (79th and 164th Infantry Regiments) and the 40th Infantry Brigade (77th and 92nd Infantry Regiments). At the end of March, 1915, the 164th Infantry Regiment was withdrawn to form part of a new 111th Division, and the remaining three regiments of the division were grouped in the 40th Infantry Brigade.

History, 1914. On mobilization, the X. Army Corps (19th and 20th Divisions) formed part of the Second German Army under General von Bülow, which entered Belgium on the left of the First Army. The X. Army Corps, under General von Emmich, distinguished itself especially early in August in the assault and capture of the fortress of Liége. The Second Army then swung southwards and advanced through Charleroi, Rethel, Reims and finally crossed the Marne. In the battle of the Marne, which followed, the Corps suffered severely at the hands of the French, was thrown back across the Marne and retired till it reached the Berry-au-Bac area, north of Reims.

1915. During the winter of 1914-1915, the X. Corps saw a certain amount of local fighting in the Berry-au-Bac area, and also sent elements to the Souain—Perthes front to reinforce the VIII. Corps. At the end of April, the Corps was transferred to the Russian front to assist in the great German summer offensive of 1915. It entrained on the 26th April at Le Chatelet and travelled *viâ* Rethel — Amagne — Sedan—Trier—Coblenz—Nassau—Giessen—Marburg—Leipzig—Dresden —Bautzen —Görlitz—Neisse—Cosel—Ratibor—Oderberg—Teschen—Jablunkau, arriving at Iglo (Hungary) after a journey of 91 hours. It was incorporated in the Eleventh German Army under General von Mackensen, which advanced into Galicia and was engaged at Radymno, Jaroslav, Przemysl and Lemberg. Thence the Army swung northwards until it had reached its final objective.

Offensive operations on the Russian front having come to a standstill, and the pressure exercised by the Allies on the Western front becoming more intense, the X. Army Corps was sent back to the Western front, arriving just in time to reinforce the Champagne front, threatened by the successful French offensive. It entrained on the 17th September at Bielostok and travelled *viâ* Liége and Malines to the Champagne, where it came into line on about the 1st October and took part in a number of counter-attacks north of Massiges. When the fighting in Champagne had subsided, the Corps was transferred to the area west of Craonne, and relieved the VII. Reserve Corps on the 28th October. No fighting worth mentioning took place during the winter that followed, and on the 15th May, 1916, the Corps was relieved by the XVIII. Corps and went to rest in the Laon area.

1916.

The successful Russian offensive, which began early in June, 1916, and broke through the Austrian defences on a wide front in the Brody—Lutsk—Kovel area, obliged the German Higher Command to send a number of divisions from France to this front as reinforcements. The X. Army Corps entrained in the Laon area on the 7th and 8th June; the 19th Division travelled *viâ* Luxemburg — Trier — Leipzig — Breslau—Lublin to Kovel, while the 20th Division took the northern route and travelled *viâ* Namur—Liége—Berlin—Posen—Warsaw—Brest Litovsk to Kovel. Here again the Corps came in for some very hard fighting and lost heavily. It succeeded, however, in conjunction with the other German divisions sent as reinforcements, in bringing the Russian advance to a standstill in the course of the summer.

Early in November, the X. Army Corps was relieved in the Kiselin area by the VIII. Army Corps and returned to France. It entrained at Turisk on the 15th November and came by the following route: Kovel—Brest Litovsk—Warsaw—Posen—Kalisch—Frankfurt a/O.—Berlin—Hannover—Münster—Dortmund—Düsseldorf—Cologne—Aachen—Liége—Namur—Hirson—Anor, detraining on the 20th November. The 20th Division then proceeded to the Trélon area and rested until the beginning of 1917. On the 5th January, the 20th Division came into line east of Moulin-sous-Touvent (Oise) and replaced the 213th Division. In March, it took part in the retirement to the Hindenburg line and was then withdrawn. On the 16th April, when the great French attack on the Aisne took place, the division engaged elements in the Troyon sector, and on the 20th April relieved the 16th Reserve Division east of Cerny-en-Laonnois. It was engaged in extremely hard fighting until the 6th May and was then replaced by the 11th Bavarian Division. After a short period of rest it came into line in a quiet sector of the Champagne, south of Tahure, where it replaced the 51st Reserve Division.

1917.

The 20th Division was not to rest in this area for long. Early in July, the Russians had successfully attacked on the Halicz front and had captured this town. Continuing their advance, they drove the Austrians out of Kalusz, and were threatening Lemberg from the south. The 20th Division was then again sent eastwards with other divisions as a reinforcement to the wavering Austrians. It was relieved in Champagne by the 41st Division on the 3rd July, and on the 10th July left for Galicia. The 20th Division first came into action south of Kalusz (Stanislau area) and assisted in holding up the Russian advance. On about the 18th July, the 20th Division took part in the Austro-German counter-offensive between Brody and the Carpathians, which forced the Russians to evacuate Galicia and part of the Bukovina. When this advance came to a standstill, the 20th Division was holding a sector north of Husiatin. It was replaced on the 17th August by the 241st Division and marched to Brzezany, where it entrained on the 23rd August for the Riga front. The division travelled *viâ* Lemberg—Cholm—Brest-Litovsk—Grodno Kovno—Mitau to Neigut, a rail journey of 80 hours. In the German offensive which commenced on the 1st September and culminated in the capture of Riga and Dünamünde, the 20th Division was not seriously engaged.

The 20th Division was withdrawn from the Riga front about the middle of September and transferred to Belgium. It arrived at Roulers on the 28th September and relieved the 4th Bavarian Division in the sector north of Zonnebeke (north-east of Ypres) on the 1st October. The division was to have taken part in an attack on the 4th October with the object of retaking Zonnebeke and the British positions in that neighbourhood. This attack, however, was forestalled by the British attack, which took place an hour earlier. In the fighting which followed, the 20th Division was completely smashed up; it lost 1,350 prisoners, taken from all the companies of the division but four, and also lost very heavily in killed and wounded.

The division was immediately withdrawn from the Flanders battle and, after a short rest, relieved the 18th Reserve Division in the Quéant sector. When the British attacked at Cambrai on the 20th November, elements of the division, reinforced by three companies of the divisional field recruit depôt, were engaged at Moeuvres (west of Cambrai), and on the 30th November elements of the 92nd and 79th Infantry Regiment assisted in the great German counter-attack on the Moeuvres—Bourlon front. In January the division was relieved by the 119th Division and went to rest in the Denain area. Early in February it returned to line in the Bullecourt—Quéant sector, relieving the 16th Bavarian Division and was withdrawn again on the 21st February on relief by the 195th Division.

1918.

Uniform. The men of the 79th Infantry Regiment wear the inscription "Gibraltar" embroidered on a blue band on their right sleeve. The regiment received this distinction in 1901 for having belonged to "The King's German Legion" from 1803 to 1816, when it fought in Spain. The helmet plate of the 77th Infantry Regiment bears the inscription "Waterloo," while that of the 92nd Infantry Regiment bears the inscription "Peninsula," and also has a death's head and cross bones in German silver.

General. The 20th Division has the reputation of being a very good division, and can be described as being one of the German Gladiator divisions, taking part in most offensive operations or assisting to re-establish the situation in threatened areas. It is composed entirely of Hanoverians, who have usually shown themselves to be reliable soldiers.

The 20th Division is commanded by Maj.-Gen. von Trautmann.

NOTE ON THE 24th DIVISION.

Composition. The 24th (2nd Saxon) Division originally formed, with the 40th (4th Saxon) Division, the XIX. (Second Royal Saxon) Army Corps, the headquarters of which are at Leipzig. The 24th Division consisted of the 47th (3rd Saxon) Infantry Brigade—139th (11th Saxon) and 179th (14th Saxon) Infantry Regiments—and the 48th (4th Saxon) Infantry Brigade—106th (7th Saxon) and 107th (8th Saxon) Infantry Regiments. In March, 1915, the 106th and 107th Infantry Regiments were withdrawn to join the newly-formed 58th Division. The 24th Division remained only a brigade strong until Christmas, 1915, when the 133rd Infantry Regiment, which had originally belonged to the 40th Division and had been attached to the 111th Division in the Arras sector, was transferred to it. The three regiments of the 24th Division were then grouped under the 47th Infantry Brigade, and later under the 89th Infantry Brigade.

History, 1914. At the beginning of the war, the XIX. Corps formed part of the Third German Army under General von Hausen, which advanced through the Ardennes and took part in the battle of Dinant. In the subsequent wheel southwards, the XIX. Corps crossed the Marne near Châlons, and reached a point some way south of that town, where the German Army was compelled to retreat to the Aisne. In the "race for the sea" at the end of October, the XIX. Corps was transferred to the Sixth Army under the Crown Prince of Bavaria. It was engaged by our cavalry and the advanced guard of our III. Corps and driven back on to the line between Ploegsteert Wood and Bois Grenier.

1915. During 1915 and the first half of 1916, the XIX. Corps as a whole was not seriously engaged. Elements of both its divisions were sent to reinforce threatened sectors of the front on various occasions, returning to the Corps sector between Ploegsteert Wood and Bois Grenier when their help was no longer required. Elements of the 24th Division were engaged at L'Epinette, east of Armentières, in January. In the battles of Neuve Chapelle in March, and Festubert in May and June, the division sent up reinforcements to support the VII. Corps.

1916. At the beginning of August, 1916, the XIX. Corps was transferred to the Somme front. The 24th Division went into line north of Pozières, relieving the 17th Reserve Division. It was engaged in severe fighting and suffered heavy losses. After spending about three weeks in line, the Corps was transferred to the Neuve Chapelle—La Bassée area, but after six weeks' rest returned to the Somme front. The 24th Division relieved the 4th Ersatz Division near Le Sars, on the 15th October, and remained in line for another spell of three weeks. Early in November, the XIX. Corps was relieved by the Guard Reserve Corps and returned to the St. Eloi—Messines area. The 24th Division went into line in the Wytschaete sector.

The losses reported by the 24th Division in the Somme battle amounted to 6,217—69 per cent. of establishment. The 133rd Infantry Regiment suffered most heavily; it lost 2,281 men, or 76 per cent. of establishment.

1917. At the beginning of May, 1917, the 24th Division was relieved by the 2nd Division and went to rest in the Mouscron area, but a few days later it returned to front line on the right of the 2nd Division. When it became evident to the German Higher Command that a British offensive was imminent on the Wytschaete—Messines front, preparations were made to withdraw the Saxon elements from line in that area. On the 31st May, the 24th Division was replaced south of the Ypres—Comines Canal by the 35th Division, not, however, before it had suffered considerably from the preliminary bombardment. It was withdrawn to Lille to rest and was still there on the 6th June, under orders to leave for Russia. Owing to the British success at Messines, these orders were countermanded. On the 7th June, the division was alarmed and sent back to Menin, whence it was brought up to hold the Oosttaverne line, which was menaced by the British advance. It relieved the 7th Division in the Hollebeke sector on the 15th June, but was withdrawn again on the arrival of the 10th Bavarian Division on the 26th June.

The 24th Division rested in the area south of Lille until the 10th-11th August, when it relieved the 18th Reserve Division in the Warneton sector. It remained in this quiet sector for two months, but sent elements to reinforce the Bavarian

Ersatz Division north of the Ypres—Menin road in the British attack on the 20th September. On the 11th October, the 24th Division, having been replaced in the Houthem sector by the 8th Division, relieved the 25th Division astride the Ypres—Menin road, and was severely engaged on the 26th October, when Gheluvelt was lost to the British, but retaken in a counter-attack. The division, which had suffered severely, was relieved on the 28th-29th October by the 18th Reserve Division, and was transferred to Artois, relieving the 38th Division south of the river Scarpe on **1918.** the 2nd November. After an uneventful three months in this sector it was replaced by the 185th Division and went to rest.

General. The 24th Division is not a good one. Its *moral*, like that of most Saxon units, is low. During 1915 and the first half of 1916, when in the Armentières sector, its attitude was entirely passive. The division fought fairly well on the Somme in 1916, and held its ground in the fighting at Gheluvelt in 1917.

The 24th Division is commanded by Major-General Hammer.

NOTE ON THE 25th DIVISION.

Composition. The 25th Division is recruited in the XVIII. Army Corps District (Hesse), which comprises the towns of Frankfurt a/M., Mainz, Darmstadt, Wiesbaden, Homburg, Giessen, Worms, Offenbach.

The 25th Division originally consisted of the 49th Infantry Brigade (115th Body Guard Infantry Regiment and 116th Infantry Regiment) and the 50th Infantry Brigade (117th Body Infantry Regiment and 118th Infantry Regiment). Early in March, 1915, the 118th Infantry Regiment was withdrawn to join a reconstituted 56th Division, and the three remaining regiments of the division were grouped in the 49th Infantry Brigade.

History, 1914. At the outbreak of war, the 25th Division formed part of the Fourth German Army under Duke Albrecht of Württemberg. It marched into France by way of Luxemburg, took part in the battle of Neufchâteau on the 22nd August, crossed the River Meuse on the 28th August and reached the Marne on the 5th September. In the battle of the Marne, on the 7th September, the 25th Division suffered a severe defeat at the hands of the French and was thrown back across the river. In the retreat which followed it was severely engaged at Crainville, Rettonvillers and Goyencourt. In October, when the great outflanking movement in the " race for the sea " took place, the 25th Division was transferred to the Roye area, where it came under the orders of the Second German Army under von Bülow.

1916. The division remained in this area until the end of January, 1916, when it was withdrawn and transferred to the Verdun front. It entrained at St. Quentin and travelled by Maubeuge—Namur and Arlon. Prior to the great offensive the division was billeted in the Danvillers area. It came into line on about the 21st February and relieved elements of the 10th Reserve Division north of the Bois des Caures.

On the 22nd February the first great attack on the Verdun front was delivered. The 25th Division, with all three regiments in line, captured the Bois des Caures, the villages of Beaumont and Louvemont, and by the 7th March reached the area south-west of Douaumont. The division was then withdrawn to rest and refit. After about five weeks it returned to the Verdun front and, on the 17th April, took part in the attack between the Bois d'Haudromont and Douaumont. The division gained very little ground and had to be relieved on the 25th April by the 6th Division. The total casualties, admitted officially, for the 25th Division at Verdun were 5,731.

After a short period of rest the 25th Division came into line in a quiet sector west of Craonne, where it relieved the 20th Division on the 15th May. In this sector the division saw very little fighting and had practically no casualties. Early in September the 25th Division was relieved by the 1st Bavarian Reserve Division in the Craonne sector, and was transferred to the Somme, where it replaced elements of the 53rd Reserve Division and 13th Division in the Bouchavesnes sector on the 15th September. The division had been brought up specially to recapture the village of Bouchavesnes and the ground lost in that area. In the attack, which was organized on a large scale, the division was quite unsuccessful and suffered severely. The division was relieved on the night of the 29th-30th by the 9th Reserve Division, and was withdrawn to the Woëvre, where it relieved the 1st Bavarian Division in the St. Mihiel sector on the 10th October. After only three weeks in this area the 1st Bavarian Division returned to the St. Mihiel front, and the 25th Division was again dispatched to the Somme. It rested in the Le Cateau area till early in December, and then relieved the 36th Division, on the 8th December, in the Pressoire—Chaulnes sector (south of the River Somme).

1917. By this time the battle of the Somme had come to a standstill and conditions reverted to ordinary trench warfare In March, 1917, when the German forces in the Somme area withdrew to a shorter line, the 25th Division came into contact with the French on several occasions, and at Savy (west of St. Quentin) lost about 100 prisoners. Early in June the division was relieved by the 12th Reserve Division and withdrawn to rest. At the beginning of July the division appeared in line again south-west of St. Quentin, replaced the 235th Division and delivered a partially successful local attack. The casualties incurred in this attack appear to have been slight, as no identifications by contact were secured.

The 25th Division was relieved by the 12th Reserve Division on the 9th September and went to rest in the neighbourhood of Origny (east of St. Quentin). On the night of the 20th-21st September the whole division entrained and came to Mouscron, whence it proceeded by light railway to Menin. The division came up into reserve on the night of the 21st and relieved the 9th Reserve Division south of the Ypres—Menin road on the 22nd. In the British attack on the 26th September the division was severely engaged and lost some ground. It was relieved by the 24th Division on the 11th October and went to rest in the area north-east of Ghent until the 15th November, when it relieved the 44th Reserve Division in the Passchendaele sector. The division alternated in this sector, doing seven days in line and six days in reserve, with the 44th Reserve Division until the 4th December, when it was relieved by the 16th Division. After ten days' rest, the 25th Division relieved the 36th Reserve Division and did one tour of duty in the sector north of Becelaere.

1918. About the middle of January, it appeared again in the Passchendaele sector, relieving the 16th Division, and remained there until the 10th February, when it was relieved by the 15th Division.

General. The 25th Division has the reputation of being a good division. It fought well at Verdun and on the Somme.

The 25th Division is commanded by Lieut.-Gen. von Dressler und Scharfenstein.

NOTE ON THE 26th DIVISION.

Composition. The 26th Division is recruited in the XIII. Army Corps District, which has its headquarters at Stuttgart, and embraces the whole of the Kingdom of Württemberg.

The 26th Division, at the outbreak of war, consisted of the 51st Infantry Brigade 119th Grenadier and 125th Infantry Regiments) and the 52nd Infantry Brigade (121st Infantry and 122nd Fusilier Regiments). In April, 1915, the 122nd Fusiliers were withdrawn to join the new 105th Division, and the remaining three regiments of the division were grouped in the 51st Infantry Brigade.

History, 1914. At the beginning of the war, the XIII. Corps (26th and 27th Divisions) formed part of the Fifth Army under the Crown Prince. It took part in the battle of Longwy, crossed the Meuse, and wheeled southwards between the Meuse and the Argonne. After the battle of the Aisne, the Corps was split up, and its two divisions remained separated for over a year.

The 27th Division remained in the Argonne, while the 26th Division was sent north to Tournai and marched with the XIX. Corps to the line Menin—Armentières. On the 16th October, it came into action against the British 7th Division between Gheluvelt and Menin. Shortly afterwards, it was combined with the 25th Reserve Division to form a reconstituted XIII. Corps, and was engaged in the Radinghem—Le Maisnil sector, south of Armentières.

Towards the end of November, the reconstituted XIII. Corps entrained for Russia, and fought under General von Fabeck on the Bzura and Ravka, in Poland. **1915.** It suffered very heavy losses. In March, 1915, the 26th Division was sent north to the Prasnysz area, and was engaged on this sector of the front in company with the 4th Guard and 3rd Divisions, which were grouped with it in another composite XIII. Corps.

In October, 1915, the 26th Division was transferred to General von Kövess's Army for the offensive against Serbia. It took part in the advance up the Lower Morava towards Kragujevatz, and towards the end of November, the task of the German contingent having been completed, was withdrawn to rest at Belgrade prior to being transported to the West. The 26th Division entrained at Semlin on the 20th November, and travelled viâ Budapest—Vienna—Munich—Ulm—Zweibrücken—Saarbrücken to Bertrix, where it detrained on the 30th November. A few days later the 27th Division entrained at Grandpré and came to the Courtrai area, where the original XIII. Corps was now concentrated.

1916. During January, 1916, the XIII. Corps relieved the XV. Corps on the south-eastern sector of the Ypres salient. The 26th Division took over the right sector, from Hooge to the south of Sanctuary Wood, with the 27th Division on its left between Sanctuary Wood and the Ypres—Comines Canal. The Corps remained on the Ypres salient from January to July. During this period the fighting on the salient was much less constant and severe than during the spring and summer of 1915. The Corps took part, however, in some hard local fighting. The XIII. Corps was more seriously engaged on the 2nd June, when troops of both divisions, reinforced by the Silesian 117th Division, violently attacked the Canadians in the Zillebeke sector after a very heavy bombardment, and captured Observatory Ridge. A counter-attack resulted in the recapture of all the lost ground. In this fighting some of the regiments of the XIII. Corps suffered very heavy losses.

At the end of July, the Corps was relieved on the Ypres salient by von Werder's Corps, and was brought to the Somme front. The 27th Division came into line about the 1st August in the Guillemont sector, and a few days later the 26th Division took up a position on its right, in front of Longueval. The whole of the Corps was opposed to the British except the extreme left of the 27th Division, which was engaged with the French. The XIII. Corps remained in line for about three weeks, during which it successfully resisted several attempts to capture the village of Guillemont. Although the Corps held its ground in these attacks, it suffered severely during its long spell in the trenches; it was throughout under heavy artillery fire, and the intense heat and rationing difficulties caused a good deal of sickness in its ranks. The XIII. Corps was relieved about the 25th August by the 56th and 111th Divisions, and replaced the XXIII. Reserve Corps in the Wytschaete sector. After spending two months and a half in that sector, it was relieved by the XIX. Corps about the 11th November, and returned to the Somme. The 27th Division was identified on the 20th November in the sector north of Sailly-Saillisel, where it had relieved the 30th Division. Shortly afterwards, the 26th Division joined it, relieving the 222nd Division in the sector south of Le Transloy on the 7th December. The 26th Division

1917. remained in line till the beginning of March, and then went into reserve in the First Army area.

At the commencement of the great British offensive at Arras in April, the 26th Division was rushed up from Army Reserve. It relieved the 3rd Bavarian Division south of the River Scarpe, and on the 14th April carried out a strong but unsuccessful counter-attack. After only a fortnight in line, it was relieved by the 9th Reserve Division, and withdrawn to rest. The 26th Division returned to its old sector south of the River Scarpe on the 31st May, and replaced the 9th Reserve Division. By this time, the heavy fighting in this area had subsided into ordinary trench warfare, in which the division suffered few losses. Towards the end of July the 17th Reserve Division, which was holding the sector on the left of the 26th Division, extended its front northwards and took over the sector south of the River Scarpe. The 26th Division was then transferred *via* Douai—Thumeries and Seclin to the Lille area, where it rested until the 15th August, when it was transported to the Ypres front. It entrained at Loos and travelled *via* Tourcoing and Courtrai to Roulers, and thence by road and light railway to Westroosebeke. On the 16th August it relieved the 79th Reserve Division and elements of the 12th Reserve Division in the sector north of Langemarck. It was not engaged in any infantry fighting on a large scale, but suffered severely from shelling. On the 4th September it was replaced by the 208th Division and went to rest in Lorraine. Here the division was equipped and trained as a mountain division and, at the end of September, was transported to the Italian front.

The 26th Division formed part of Otto von Below's 14th Army, which broke through the Julian front towards the end of October. Later, the 26th Division was engaged in heavy fighting on the River Tagliamento, receiving a special mention in the German communiqué for its performance. In November the division was withdrawn to the Trentino and, during December, returned to Alsace.

General. The 26th Division, which has seen a great deal of fighting since the beginning of the war, is a thoroughly good division, and has nearly always acquitted itself well. There is evidence that the severe handling which they received before Ypres in June, 1916, and on the Somme in August caused—temporarily, at any rate—a deterioration in the *moral* of some of the regiments. At Ypres, in 1917, the *moral* of the division was badly shaken by artillery fire and by the trying circumstances in front line.

Maj.-Gen. Duke Ulrich von Württemberg commands the 26th Division.

NOTE ON THE 27th DIVISION.

Composition. The XIII. (Royal Württemberg) Corps consists of the 26th and 27th Divisions. Its headquarters are at Stuttgart, and the Corps District embraces the whole of the Kingdom of Württemberg.

The 27th Division originally consisted of the 53rd Infantry Brigade (123rd Grenadier and 124th Infantry Regiments) and the 54th Infantry Brigade (120th and 127th Infantry Regiments). The 127th Infantry Regiment was withdrawn early in 1917 to join a new 242nd Division, and the remaining three regiments of the division were grouped in the 53rd Infantry Brigade.

History, 1914. At the beginning of the war the XIII. Corps formed part of the Fifth Army under the Crown Prince. It took part in the battle of Longwy, crossed the Meuse and wheeled southwards, between the Meuse and the Argonne. After the battle of the Aisne the corps was split up and its two divisions remained separated for over a year. The 27th Division remained in the Argonne, while the 26th Division was sent north to Tournai and marched with the XIX. Corps to the line Menin—Armentières.

1915. Throughout the year 1915 the 27th Division remained in the Argonne. It was constantly engaged in mine warfare, and in August, 1915, took part in the unsuccessful offensive of the Crown Prince's Army. In the following month elements of the 53rd Infantry Brigade were sent to Champagne to act as reserves during the French offensive. In December, 1915, the 27th Division entrained at Grandpré and came to the Courtrai area, where the original XIII. Corps was now concentrated.

1916. During January, 1916, the XIII. Corps relieved the XV. Corps on the southeastern sector of the Ypres salient. The 26th Division took over the right sector, from Hooge to the south of Sanctuary Wood, with the 27th Division on its left, between Sanctuary Wood and the Ypres—Comines Canal. The corps remained on the Ypres salient from January to July. During this period the fighting on the salient was much less constant and severe than during the spring and summer of 1915. The corps took part, however, in some hard local fighting. On the 14th February troops of the 27th Division captured some British trenches at the "Bluff," just north of the Ypres—Comines Canal, but these were retaken on the 2nd March. The 123rd Grenadiers suffered heavily on this occasion. The XIII. Corps was more seriously engaged on the 2nd June, when troops of both divisions, reinforced by the Silesian 117th Division, violently attacked the Canadians in the Zillebeke sector, after a very heavy bombardment, and captured Observatory Ridge. A counter-attack resulted in the recapture of all the lost ground. In this fighting some of the regiments of the XIII. Corps suffered very heavy losses.

At the end of July the corps was relieved on the Ypres salient by von Werder's Corps, and was brought to the Somme front. The 27th Division came into line about the 1st August, in the Guillemont sector, and a few days later the 26th Division took up a position on its right, in front of Longueval. The whole of the corps was opposed to the British except the extreme left of the 27th Division, which was engaged with the French. The XIII. Corps remained in line for about three weeks, during which it successfully resisted several attempts to capture the village of Guillemont. Although the corps held its ground in these attacks, it suffered severely during its long spell in the trenches; it was throughout under heavy artillery fire, and the intense heat and rationing difficulties caused a good deal of sickness in its ranks.

The XIII. Corps was relieved about the 25th August by the 56th and 111th Divisions and replaced the XXIII. Reserve Corps in the Wytschaete sector. After spending two months and a half in that sector, it was relieved by the XIX. Corps about the 11th November and returned to the Somme. The 27th Division was identified on the 20th November in the sector north of Sailly-Saillisel, where it had relieved the 30th Division. Shortly afterwards the 26th Division joined it, relieving the 222nd Division in the sector south of Le Transloy on the 7th December.

1917. The 27th Division was relieved by the 22nd Reserve Division early in February and, after resting for a month in the Caudry area, returned to the Somme front to relieve the 26th Division. It took part in the early stage of the retreat, and towards the end of March was relieved by the 199th Division in the Villers-Faucon area. After a short rest it came into line again in the Croisilles sector, relieving the 26th Reserve Division. The 27th Division saw some hard fighting around Bullecourt during April and suffered severely. It was relieved on the 6th May by the 3rd Guard Division and, after a short period of rest, came into line in the Honnecourt—Banteux sector, south of Cambrai, where it relieved the 22nd Reserve Division on the 22nd May.

The 27th Division was relieved south of Cambrai by the 10th Bavarian Division on the 11th August. It was not seriously engaged during the ten weeks it spent in this quiet sector and was withdrawn from line as a comparatively fresh division. The 27th Division then followed its sister division, the 26th, to Flanders and relieved the 5th Bavarian Division in the Passchendaele sector, north-east of Ypres, on about the 23rd August. It entrained at Caudry on the 12th August and travelled *via* Lille—Tourcoing and Menin to Ledeghem, whence it marched to Roulers. The division remained in reserve in this area until the 24th August and then came into line in the St. Julien sector, replacing the 12th Reserve Division. Although it was not engaged in any fighting on a large scale, the division suffered severely from artillery fire, and was relieved on the 12th-13th September by the 2nd Guard Reserve Division. To recover from its losses the division was sent to rest in the area north-east of Ghent. After about a month in this area, the 27th Division was again called upon to take part in the battle of Ypres, and relieved the 18th Division north of Langemarck on the 11th October. After a week in the line the 27th Division was relieved by elements of the 26th Reserve and 58th Divisions, but returned to the same sector again on the 24th. The Flanders fighting was drawing to a close by this time, and about the 12th November the 27th Division was withdrawn from the Ypres front. Entraining at Ghent, it was transferred to Alsace, travelling *via* Brussels—Namur—Arlon—Luxemburg — Diedenhofen — Metz — Zabern — Colmar — Mülhausen — Bartenheim. The division detrained at the last-named place and marched to Kötzingen. About ten days later the 27th Division moved from Mülhausen to the Colmar area, and rested at Riedwihr from the 10th December until the beginning of February, 1918. On the **1918.** 2nd February the division left Colmar, arriving at Cambrai on the 4th. It came into line in the Graincourt sector on the 6th, relieving the 24th Reserve Division.

General. The 27th Division has fought well since the beginning of the war. There is evidence that the severe handling which it received before Ypres in June, 1916, and on the Somme in August, caused—temporarily, at any rate—a deterioration in the *moral* of some of the regiments. The 27th Division may be regarded, however, as a thoroughly good unit, one of the best in the German Army as it is to-day.

The 27th Division is commanded by Major-General von Maur.

NOTE ON THE 30th DIVISION.

Composition. On taking the field, the 30th Division formed, with the 39th Division, the XV. Army Corps. This corps has its headquarters at Strassburg, and is nominally recruited in Alsace, although most of its units also receive drafts from other army corps districts, while the 105th Infantry Regiment (30th Division) is an entirely Saxon unit.

The 30th Division originally consisted of the 60th Infantry Brigade (99th and 143rd Infantry Regiments) and the 85th Infantry Brigade (105th and 136th Infantry Regiments). In March, 1915, the 136th Infantry Regiment was withdrawn to form part of a new 115th Division, and the three remaining infantry regiments were grouped together in the 60th Infantry Brigade.

History, 1914.
At the beginning of the war the XV. Corps formed part of the Seventh Army (von Heeringen), which advanced through the Northern Vosges, but failed to break through the defences of the Upper Moselle. Early in October the corps was transferred to the area north of Reims, where it remained about a month. It was then rushed up to Flanders, where it took part in the heavy fighting subsequent to the first battle of Ypres. The corps was then holding the front between the Ypres—Menin road and the Ypres—Comines Canal.

1915.
During the whole of 1915 the XV. Corps was almost continuously engaged in local fighting. In the battle, which began on the 17th April around Hill 60 (south-east of Ypres), the 105th Infantry Regiment suffered particularly heavy casualties and lost a number of prisoners. The corps took no active part in the second battle of Ypres, but advanced its line as far as Hooge, when the British forces withdrew to a shorter line after the battle. During July and August there was some heavy local fighting at Hooge.

1916.
During January, 1916, the XV. Corps was gradually relieved south-east of Ypres by the XIII. Corps. Between the 23rd and 30th January it entrained at Courtrai, travelled *viâ* Ath—Mons—Charleroi—Namur—Libramont—Arlon—Luxemburg to Aumetz and came into line in the Etain—Damloup sector, east of Verdun, on or about the 20th February. It remained in line in this area for about eight months. It was engaged in the Verdun battle immediately upon its arrival. At the outset the corps was able to advance its line a considerable distance into the Woëvre plain, but was brought to a standstill when it had reached the Hauts de Meuse. The 105th Regiment, which was in divisional reserve, was called upon to reinforce the III. Army Corps, and took part in the attack on the Bois de Chauffour, in the Douaumont sector, on the 26th February. During June and the following months elements of the corps were severely handled by the French in the fighting around Vaux Fort and the Thiaumont Work.

The total casualties, admitted officially, for the 30th Division in the battle of Verdun were 150 officers and 8,259 other ranks.

Early in October, when the fighting on the Verdun front had practically ceased, the XV. Corps was relieved by the 19th Ersatz Division. It entrained between the 3rd and 10th October at Baroncourt and came *viâ* Sedan and Hirson to the Valenciennes area.

On the 25th-28th October the corps relieved the 1st and 2nd Bavarian Divisions in the Sailly-Saillisel sector, north of the Somme. Bitter fighting took place here. The French drove the corps from its positions, captured part of the village of Sailly-Saillisel and took about 390 prisoners of the 30th Division. The corps was withdrawn from the Somme about the middle of November and was transferred to the area north of Verdun to rest and refit. The 39th Division went into line early in December, and the 30th Division replaced it on the 21st in the Haudromont sector.

1917.
The 30th Division remained here until the 27th February, 1917, when it changed places with the 25th Reserve Division from the area east of Auberive. It was engaged here on the 17th April in the Champagne battle, but, being on the flank of the attack, did not suffer to any extent. The 30th Division remained in line here until the end of August, when it was transferred to the Verdun area, and came into line west of the Meuse on the 25th, relieving the 48th Reserve Division. The French offensive in this area was now concluded, and the 30th Division was not heavily engaged. It held the sector until the end of October, when it was relieved and, after a short rest, transferred to the Laon area. On the 20th November, when the British attacked near Cambrai, the 30th Division was sent up to reinforce this front. It entrained near Laon on the 21st November and detrained at Wambaix and Cattenières. It took an important part in the German counter-attacks of the 30th November and, on that day and on the 1st December, made a series of violent attacks on Masnières. Nine separate attacks were repulsed before the British finally evacuated the place in order to effect an improvement in the line. The 30th Division was relieved in the Masnières sector at the end of December and during January,

1918.
1918, rested in the Sedan area. On about the 9th February it relieved the 28th Reserve Division in Eastern Champagne.

General.
The *moral* of the 30th Division can be described as good. It has seen a great deal of fighting, and has always acquitted itself well.

The 30th Division is commanded by Maj.-Gen. Graf Lamsdorf.

NOTE ON THE 31st DIVISION.

Composition.
The 31st Division is recruited in the Saarbrücken district (Lorraine), and at the outbreak of war formed, with the 42nd Division, the XXI. Army Corps. It consisted, when it took the field in 1914, of the 32nd Infantry Brigade (70th and 174th Infantry Regiments) and the 62nd Infantry Brigade (137th and 166th Infantry Regiments).

In the spring of 1915, the 137th Infantry Regiment was transferred to the newly-formed 108th Division, and the three remaining regiments were grouped under the staff of the 32nd Infantry Brigade.

History, 1914.   The XXI. Corps, on mobilization, was included in the Sixth Army under the Crown Prince of Bavaria, which invaded French Lorraine, but was held up in front of Nancy. When, after the retreat to the Aisne, the 6th Army was transferred from Lorraine to Artois, the 31st Division, with its sister division, was transferred to the Second Army in Picardy. The 31st Division was engaged in the Chaulnes sector,

1915.   south of Péronne. In February, 1915, the two divisions of the XXI. Corps were transferred to the Eastern front and allotted to the Eighth (later the Tenth) Army under von Eichhorn, on the East Prussian frontier. In the great summer offensive of 1915 the Tenth Army, on the left flank, maintained a passive attitude until after the capture of Warsaw at the end of July; it then advanced rapidly, taking Kovno and

1916-17.   Vilna, but was brought to a standstill in the autumn just east of the latter place. When the front became stationary, the 31st Division took up a position in the Lake Narotch sector, south of Dvinsk, where it remained until the middle of December, 1917. The Narotch sector was a very quiet one, and the division was never seriously engaged there.

On the 5th December, the 31st Division was relieved by the 226th Division, and went to rest at Vilna. On the 16th December, the division entrained and travelled *viâ* Wirballen — Eydtkuhnen — Insterburg — Königsberg — Elbing—Marienburg—Dirschau—Konitz—Neustettin— Stargard—Stettin—Pasewalk—Neu Brandenburg—Güstrow—Hamburg—Bremen—Osnabrück—Münster—Essen—Crefeld—Gladbach—Aachen—Visé—Tongres—Hasselt—Aerschot—Louvain—Malines—Moerbeke (north-east of Ghent), where it detrained on the 21st December, after a journey of 120

1918.   hours. After three weeks' hard training in this area the 31st Division came into line in the Moorslede sector on the Ypres salient, and relieved the 12th Reserve Division. It alternated in this sector with the 12th Reserve Division, doing a fortnight in line and a fortnight out resting, until the beginning of March, when it was replaced by the 15th Division and went to rest in the Courtrai area. On the 13th March, a party of three officers and 60 men were sent forward from Courtrai to carry out a raid in the Houthem sector, held at that time by the 17th Reserve Division.

General.   The 31st Division consists of three active regiments, and should be a good fighting unit; but it has had no experience at all of present-day conditions on the Western front. The division contains a number of Alsatians, who are willing to desert whenever an opportunity occurs.

The 31st Division is commanded by Maj.-Gen. von Wissel.

NOTE ON THE 32nd DIVISION.

Composition.   The 32nd Division is recruited in the XII. Army Corps District (Saxony). The principal towns in this district are Dresden, Bautzen, Zittau, Freiberg, Löbau, Meissen, Oschatz, Pirna.

On mobilization, the 32nd Division consisted of the 63rd Infantry Brigade (102nd and 103rd Infantry Regiments) and the 64th Infantry Brigade (177th and 178th Infantry Regiments). In April, 1915, the 178th Infantry Regiment was withdrawn to join a new 123rd Division, and the remaining three regiments were grouped in the 63rd Infantry Brigade.

History, 1914-15.   On the outbreak of war the 32nd Division formed part of the 3rd German Army under General von Hausen and was engaged on the right bank of the Meuse, between Namur and Neufchâteau. It fought in the Châlons sector in the battle of the Marne. The division was then transferred to the 7th German Army under General von Heeringen, and took part in the fighting near Reims; when trench warfare began, it took up its position in the Berry-au-Bac sector, north-west of Reims, and remained there till July, 1916. Early in January, 1915, the 1st Battalion of the 177th Infantry Regiment was sent to the Tahure sector in Champagne to reinforce the 16th Division. This battalion had rejoined the 32nd Division by the end of the month.

1916.   At the beginning of the successful Franco-British offensive on the Somme in July, 1916, the German Higher Command, having used up all the divisions in reserve at its disposal, was obliged to " milk " the majority of divisions in line between the battle area and Champagne to obtain a force to stop the gaps in its line south of the river. In response to this demand for reinforcements, the 32nd Division sent up the 3rd Battalion of the 102nd Infantry Regiment, which was engaged in the Belloy sector from the 3rd to the 8th July. About the 20th July, the 32nd Division was withdrawn from line north-west of Reims. Two of its regiments, the 102nd and 103rd, together with the 100th Grenadier Regiment, from the 23rd Division, and the 12th *Jäger* Battalion were combined to form a composite formation called " Frank's Division," and were transferred to the Somme. This division came into line in the Deniecourt—Vermandovillers sector at the end of July and saw very severe fighting. On the 4th September, the 177th Infantry Regiment, which had remained behind in the Berry-au-Bac area, joined up with the 102nd and 103rd Infantry Regiments, and the 32nd Division then again assumed its normal composition. The division was relieved on the 7th September and transferred to Argonne. The total casualties, admitted officially, for the engagement of the 32nd Division on the Somme were 6,218, 62 per cent. of establishment.

In Argonne, the 32nd Division replaced elements of 4th Division. On the 2nd November, the division was relieved by elements of the 9th Reserve Division and the 28th Reserve Division, and returned to the Somme. It entrained at Grandpré on 3rd November and came by rail to Hirson, whence it marched by easy stages to the area north of St. Quentin. The 32nd Division relieved the 8th Ersatz Division in the Bouchavesnes—Clery-sur-Somme sector on the 18th November. It was not seriously engaged in this sector, although in a local attack made by British troops

1917. on the 4th March, 1917, the division lost 177 prisoners. Towards the end of March the division took part in the early stages of the withdrawal of the German forces on the Somme to the Hindenburg line, and was then replaced by the 9th Reserve Division.

·When the French offensive in Champagne began, the 32nd Division, which had been resting at the Sissonne camp since the end of March, was rushed up to the sector north-west of Auberive, where it replaced the 214th Division on the 18th April. As it was withdrawn again on the following day, it can be deduced that its losses were very severe. The 32nd Division next appeared in the quiet sector at Tahure (Champagne), where it had relieved the 54th Reserve Division.

Towards the middle of June, the 54th Reserve Division returned to its old sector, and the 32nd Division was withdrawn to rest. It entrained on the 10th-11th August at Neuflize, and travelled to Flanders *via* Charleville—Maubeuge—Valenciennes—Lille—Menin—Ledeghem, where it detrained. Thence it marched to Gheluwe, and became the " counter-attack division " of the Becelaere sector. On the 24th August it came into line and made a vigorous counter-attack on Inverness Copse. After this attack, which was only partially successful, the division should have been withdrawn, but as the 34th Division, holding the sector, was quite exhausted, it remained and took the place of that division. On the 2nd September, the division was relieved by the Bavarian Ersatz Division, and transferred to the Warneton sector. The 32nd

1918. Division remained in line in this sector until the 15th January, 1918, when it was relieved by the 49th Reserve Division. It suffered rather heavily from our gas projections on the 18th-19th September. 33 men were buried at Bousbecque, the majority of them belonging to the 103rd Infantry Regiment. The stay of the division in this neighbourhood was otherwise uneventful.

General. The 32nd Division is probably one of the best Saxon divisions. The *moral* of the men is fairly good, and, although their attitude is nearly always passive, they usually counter-attack with plenty of vigour.

The 32nd Division is commanded by Maj.-Gen. von der Decken.

NOTE ON THE 34th DIVISION.

Composition. The 34th Division originally formed, with the 33rd Division, the XVI. (Metz) Army Corps. It is, however, largely recruited in Westphalia. On the outbreak of war it consisted of the 68th Infantry Brigade (67th and 145th Infantry Regiments) and the 86th Infantry Brigade (30th and 173rd Infantry Regiments). It retained its four-regiment organization until October, 1916, when the 173rd Regiment was withdrawn to join the newly-formed 223rd Division. The remaining three regiments were then grouped under the 68th Infantry Brigade.

History, 1914. At the opening of hostilities, the 34th Division formed part of the Fifth Army under the German Crown Prince, which invaded France by way of Longwy, advanced to between Châlons and Verdun, and after the battle of the Marne took up a position in the Argonne.

1915. The 34th Division remained in the Argonne for nearly two years. It took part in the unsuccessful offensives in January and July, 1915, and suffered heavy losses. Its

1916. casualties in the July attacks amounted to 900. During 1916, no infantry fighting took place in the Argonne, and the casualties of the division were slight.

In the middle of August, 1916, the 34th Division was relieved by the Alpine Corps and transferred to the Verdun front, where it came into line at the end of August in the Thiaumont sector. During September, it took part in the hard local fighting in the region of Fleury village and the Thiaumont Work. Its losses were considerable, especially in the French attack north of Fleury on the 20th September.

At the beginning of October, the 145th Regiment was transferred to the Argonne, the rest of the division remaining in line on the Verdun front. In the great French attack on the 24th October, which resulted in the recapture of the Fort Douaumont and the Thiaumont Work, the elements of the 34th Division in line offered only a feeble resistance and suffered heavy losses. The division was withdrawn from the Verdun front a few days later and was sent to a quiet sector in the Vosges. On the 14th December, elements of the division were reviewed by the Emperor near Mörchingen (Lorraine).

1917. Early in February, 1917, the 34th Division returned to the Argonne, but was withdrawn about the middle of March and transferred to the area north of Reims. During the French offensive on the 16th April and following days the division was not engaged as a whole, but sent two regiments (the 67th and 30th) to support the 43rd Reserve Division in the Brimont sector, while the 145th Regiment reinforced the 29th Division in the Champagne battle zone. In these engagements the units of the division suffered heavy losses; the 30th Infantry Regiment lost five-sixths of its strength, while the 145th Infantry Regiment lost one-third of its effectives in a counter-attack east of Mt. Cornillet. On the 25th April, the 34th Division relieved the 43rd Reserve Division in the Brimont sector, where it was not heavily engaged. It remained in line till the 21st July. During this period certain troops of the division incurred the displeasure of the Higher Command by fraternizing with the French opposite them, and were transferred to another sector as a punishment.

On the 21st July, the 34th Division was relieved by the 231st Division, rested for about a fortnight, and was then transferred to Flanders. It entrained at Neuflize (east of Le Chatelet) on the 7th August and travelled *viâ* Le Chatelet—Rethel—Charleville—Namur—Brussels—Courtrai to Ledeghem, whence the division marched to the Dadizeele area. It remained in reserve in this area till the 12th August, and then relieved the 52nd Reserve Division and elements of the 9th Reserve Division astride the Ypres—Menin road. In this sector, of the utmost importance to the Germans, extraordinarily heavy fighting developed. The division lost a certain amount of ground, including part of Inverness Copse, and had very heavy casualties. It was relieved by the 32nd Division on the 24th August and withdrawn to the Woëvre, where it relieved the 11th Division south-east of Thiaucourt on about the 18th September.

Early in November, the 34th Division was relieved in the Woëvre by the 195th Division and, shortly afterwards, was transferred to Champagne. It was in reserve near Juniville at the time of the British attack in the Cambrai area, and, on the 22nd November, the division entrained at Rethel and travelled *viâ* Hirson and Le Cateau to Caudry. Thence it marched *viâ* Cambrai to Walincourt and came into line on the 25th, when it relieved the 9th Reserve Division in the Banteux sector. On the 30th, the day of the big German counter-blow, the 34th Division, supported by a regiment of the 208th Division and with the 28th Division on its right, carried out an attack against Villers-Guislain, which was in the main successful. At the same time, it cost the 34th Division considerable losses (100 prisoners), and it was relieved on the following day by the 9th Reserve Division. It went to rest for three

1918. weeks in the Sains-Richaumont area and early in January, 1918, it relieved the 3rd Bavarian Division in the Trucy sector, south of Laon. The 34th Division was witdrawn from line at the end of February.

General. The 34th Division has excellent traditions which in the early battles in the Argonne it fully sustained. In the autumn of 1916, in common with other units on the Verdun front, it suffered a temporary collapse of *moral*, but it fought well in April, 1917, near Reims and in Champagne. At Ypres, in August, 1917, entrusted with the defence of a most important sector, it did not realize the hopes placed in it. The *moral* of the prisoners captured was distinctly poor. At Cambrai, at the end of November, it fought with some vigour.

The 34th Division is commanded by Maj.-Gen. Tetzmann.

NOTE ON THE 35th DIVISION.

Composition. The 35th Division is recuited in the XVII. Corps District, and has its headquarters at Thorn. The XVII. Corps District comprises the towns of Danzig, Thorn, Graudenz, Preussisch-Stargard and Hammerstein.

The 35th Division originally consisted of the 70th Infantry Brigade (21st and 61st Infantry Regiments) and the 87th Infantry Brigade (141st and 176th Infantry Regiments). About March, 1915, the 21st Infantry Regiment was withdrawn and sent to join the 105th Reconstituted Division, while the remaining three regiments, *i.e.*, the 61st, 141st and 176th Infantry Regiments, were grouped together in the 87th Infantry Brigade.

History, 1914. The XVII. Army Corps, consisting of the 35th and 36th Divisions, on taking the field in August, 1914, was sent to East Prussia, where it joined the Eighth German Army under von Hindenburg. With this Army it took part in the battle of Tannenberg on the 30th August, and the battle of Lötzen on the 9th September. Towards the end of September, the XVII. Corps was transferred by rail to Upper Silesia, which was being threatened by the advance of the Russian armies. Here the corps joined the Ninth German Army under von Mackensen, and took part in the second German offensive. It was engaged in the fighting at Radom on the 6th October, and took part in the advance on Warsaw and subsequent retreat. In the battle of Lodz, which took place between the 23rd November and the 6th December, the Corps was heavily engaged and suffered severely.

1915. During the winter of 1914-15, the XVII. Army Corps was in line on the Bzura front, where continuous and heavy fighting took place. In the great offensive and the advance which followed, it took an active part in the fighting on the Narew. In August, it formed part of von Gallwitz's Army Detachment, and was engaged on the right bank of the Bug and in the subsequent fighting, early in September, on the River Chtchara.

When the German advance had been brought to a standstill by the Russian forces and by the pressure exercised by the Franco-British offensive on the Western front, the XVII. Army Corps was withdrawn and transferred to France. It entrained on the 6th October at Grodno, and travelled *via* Alexandrovo—Allenstein—Posen—Berlin—Cologne—Aachen—Liége—Brussels—Audenarde—Courtrai—Lille—Douai—Cambrai, detraining at Péronne on the 10th October. It rested in the Ham area till the 16th October, when it came into line in the Roye sector, holding the Lihons—River Avre front.

1916.   The XVII. Army Corps was not seriously engaged in 1916 until the battle of the Somme. At the commencement of the battle, elements of the 35th Division were sent to reinforce threatened sectors, and units of the 176th Regiment sustained heavy casualties on the 20th July. The division was not engaged as a complete unit till September, when it was engaged on the Vermandovillers—Chilly front from the 4th-17th September, and sustained heavy losses. The total casualties officially admitted, for the period that the 35th Division was engaged in the Somme battle amount to 6,102, or 68 per cent. of the effectives engaged. The 176th Regiment incurred particularly severe losses, 101 per cent. of its effectives being officially admitted casualties.

On the 18th September, the division was withdrawn and went to Ham to refit. After a month's rest the 35th Division relieved the 36th Division on its old front, coming into line between the 15th Reserve Division and the 23rd Division on the 19th-20th October, 1916.

1917.   The 35th Division took part in the retreat of the 17th March, and by the 24th March was in line south-west of St. Quentin between the 25th and 36th Divisions. A few days before the British offensive at Arras commenced, the 35th Division was relieved by the 235th Division and, after a brief rest in the Guise area, came into line again on the 13th-14th April south-east of Arras, where it relieved the 18th Reserve Division. Only 11 days were spent in line in the Guémappe—Chérisy sector, but there is no doubt that the division suffered 50 per cent. casualties during this period as the result of our offensive. On the 25th April, it was relieved by the 199th Division, and went into rest in the Lille area.

After a little more than a month's rest, the 35th Division relieved the 24th Division south of the Ypres—Comines Canal. The division suffered exceptionally heavy losses in this sector, where it was exposed to the artillery preparation for six days, and on the 7th June was completely shattered by the British attack on the Wytschaete—Messines Ridge. Its total casualties in this battle are estimated at from five to six thousand; 1,272 prisoners alone remained in the hands of the British. The 9th Company of the 141st Infantry Regiment came out of action only six strong. The remnants of the division were relieved on the 8th June by the 7th Division and withdrawn to refit in the Cambrai area. On the 21st June, the 35th Division went into line in the Bellicourt—Bellenglise sector, a quiet part of the line north of St. Quentin, where it relieved the 111th Division.

While in line in the Bellicourt—Bellenglise sector, the 35th Division was engaged on several occasions in some hard local fighting. On the 9th July, the 176th Infantry Regiment lost 36 prisoners in a British raid. Six weeks later, the 141st Infantry Regiment lost 90 prisoners in an attack carried out by the British north-west of Hargicourt, and in the counter-attacks, carried out subsequently, lost over 50 per cent. of its strength. The division was due to be relieved at the end of August and sent to Ypres, but the losses incurred on the 26th August rendered it unfit for any battle sector. About the middle of October, having recovered sufficiently from its losses, the division was withdrawn north of St. Quentin, and transported to Flanders. On the 25th October, it appeared in the Houthulst Forest sector, and relieved the 58th Division. On the following day it was engaged in a French attack, lost some ground and a number of prisoners. It was relieved on the 4th November by the 58th Division, and then continued to alternate with this division in this sector, doing a week in line

1918.   and a week in reserve, until the 22nd January, 1918, when it was relieved by the 53rd Reserve Division, and went to rest in the Maldegem area. After a month's rest and training, it came into line again north of Ypres, replacing the 26th Reserve Division in the Merckem sector on the 18th February.

General.   The *moral* of the 35th Division, which, previous to the battle of Messines, in 1917, was good, suffered considerably owing to the enormous losses incurred, and the subsequent drafts of 1918 class recruits. A certain Polish element may be met with whose fighting qualities are decidedly inferior to the average German, and whose tendency to desert is far greater.

The 35th Division is commanded by Maj.-Gen. von Kemnitz.

NOTE ON THE 36th DIVISION.

Composition.   The 36th Division is recruited in the XVII. Army Corps District and has its headquarters at Danzig. The XVII. Army Corps District comprises the towns of Danzig, Thorn, Graudenz, Kulm, Preussisch-Stargard.

The 36th Division originally consisted of the 69th Infantry Brigade (129th and 175th Infantry Regiments) and the 71st Infantry Brigade (5th Grenadier Regiment and 128th Infantry Regiment). About the end of March, 1915, the 129th Infantry

Regiment was withdrawn to join a new 105th Division and the remaining three regiments were grouped together in the 71st Infantry Brigade.

History, 1914.
The XVII. Army Corps, consisting of the 35th and 36th Divisions, on taking the field in August, 1914, was sent to East Prussia where it joined the Eighth German Army under von Hindenburg. With this Army it took part in the battle of Tannenberg on the 30th August, and the battle of Lötzen on the 9th September. Towards the end of September, the XVII. Corps was transferred by rail to Upper Silesia which was being threatened by the advance of the Russian Armies. Here the Corps joined the Ninth German Army under von Mackensen, and took part in the second German offensive. It was engaged in the fighting at Radom on the 6th October and took part in the advance on Warsaw and subsequent retreat. In the battle of Lodz, which took place between the 23rd November and the 6th December, the Corps was heavily engaged and suffered severely.

1915.
During the winter of 1914-15 the XVII. Army Corps was in line on the Bzura front, where continuous and heavy fighting took place. In the great offensive, and the advance which followed, it took an active part in the fighting on the Narew. In August, it formed part of von Gallwitz's Army Detachment and was engaged on the right bank of the Bug and in the subsequent fighting, early in September, on the Rivier Chtchara.

When the German advance had been brought to a standstill by the Russian forces, and by the pressure exercised by the Franco-British offensive on the Western front, the XVII. Army Corps was withdrawn and transferred to France. It entrained on the 6th October at Grodno and travelled *viâ* Alexandrovo—Allenstein—Posen—Berlin—Cologne—Aachem—Liége—Brussels—Audenarde—Courtrai—Lille—Douai—Cambrai, detraining at Péronne on the 10th October. It rested in the Ham area till the 16th October, when it came into line in the Roye sector, holding the Lihons—River Avre front.

1916.
The XVII. Army Corps was not seriously engaged in 1916 until the battle of the Somme. At the commencement of the battle, elements of the 36th Division were sent to reinforce threatened sectors south of the River Somme. The 36th Division was not engaged as a complete unit until October, when the battle-front was extended to the Chaulnes—Chilly sector. In the fighting which ensued, it suffered severely and was relieved by the 35th Division on the 19th-20th October. After a short period of rest in the Nesle area, the division came into line again in the Ablaincourt sector, where it remained until the 8th December, when its place was taken by the 25th Division and itself was transferred to the Fouquescourt sector (north of Roye).

1917.
The 36th Division took part in the retreat to the Hindenburg line, which commenced on the 17th March, and by the 24th March was in line south of St. Quentin, between the 35th Division and 44th Reserve Division. On the 12th April, a few days after the British offensive at Arras had commenced, the 36th Division was relieved by the 12th Reserve Division, and, after a brief rest in the St. Quentin area, came into line on the 8th-9th May in the Guémappe sector (south-east of Arras), where it relieved the 221st Division. By this time the fighting on the Arras front had died down, and only local fighting occurred, in which the division did not suffer severely. The 36th Division was relieved by the 17th Reserve Division on the 6th June, and went to rest in the area north of Douai. It spent ten days near Thumeries and a fortnight around Raimbeaucourt. On the 3rd July the division proceeded to Cuincy (west of Douai), and, on the 4th, relieved the 5th Bavarian Division in the Oppy—Gavrelle sector. The division was not seriously engaged in this sector. Some casualties, however, were suffered at the end of July from British gas projectors. The trench strength of a company of the 128th Infantry Regiment was reduced to 25 owing to these casualties. It was relieved towards the end of August by the 214th Division and was transferred to Flanders.

The 36th Division entrained at Douai on the 28th August and travelled by Lille—Roubaix—Courtrai to Iseghem, where it arrived on the same day. It remained in reserve in this area until the 10th September and was then brought in 'busses *viâ* Rumbeke—Roulers—Oostnieuwkerke to Westroosebeke. On the night of the 10th-11th September the division was put into line north-east of St. Julien and relieved the 204th Division. At first the casualties of the division were not heavy, but on the 20th September it met the full shock of the British attack and suffered so severely that it had to be replaced on the night of the 20th-21st by the 234th Division.

To enable the division to recover from its severe losses it was transferred to a quiet sector. It left Flanders on the 25th September and on the night of the 27th-28th came into line west of St. Quentin, replacing the 233rd Division. On the 20th November, when the British attacked successfully at Cambrai, two resting battalions were sent to this area to reinforce the battle front, pending the arrival of larger rein-
1918.
forcements. Early in January, 1918, the 36th Division was relieved by the 45th Reserve Division and went to rest in the Marcy area. It returned to line at the end of January and relieved the 238th Division in the sector south of St. Quentin.

General.
The 36th Division, which fought well on the Somme in 1916, and at Arras in 1917, showed very little fight at Ypres, and the *moral* of the officers and men was bad.

A certain Polish element may be met with whose fighting qualities are decidedly inferior to the average German, and whose tendency to desert or surrender is far greater.

NOTE ON THE 38th DIVISION.

Composition.   The 38th Division is recruited in the XI. Army Corps District, which comprises the towns of Cassel, Erfurt, Eisenach, Weimar, Jena, Gotha, Coburg, Gera, etc.

The 38th Division originally consisted of the 76th Infantry Brigade (71st and 95th Infantry Regiments) and the 83rd Infantry Brigade (94th and 96th Infantry Regiments). In April, 1915, the 71st Infantry Regiment was withdrawn to join a new 103rd Division, and the remaining three regiments were grouped in the 83rd Infantry Brigade.

History, 1914.   At the beginning of the war, the 38th Division, together with the 22nd Division, formed the XI. Army Corps. This Army Corps was incorporated in the Third German Army under General von Hausen, which advanced through the Ardennes and took part in the battle of Dinant. At the end of August, the XI. Army Corps was withdrawn from Belgium and transferred to Silesia, whence it took part in the invasion of Southern Poland. The Army Group of which it formed part was outflanked and compelled to retire on the Plock-Lodz front. In November, it was transferred to the Ninth Army under von Mackensen and, in the following month, to the Tenth. It took part in the severe fighting in the Skernevitsi area, south-west of Warsaw, in the winter of 1914-15.

1915.   Early in 1915, the XI. Corps again formed part of the Ninth Army, now under General von Fabeck, and saw fighting in the Rava-Ruska area. Shortly afterwards, the XI. Army Corps, such as it was on mobilization, was broken up; the 22nd Division was transferred to the Eleventh Army (von Mackensen) operating in Southern Poland, and the 38th Division joined von Gallwitz's Army Detachment north of Warsaw.

The 38th Division then took part in the great German summer offensive of 1915 and saw a great deal of hard fighting. Towards the end of September the division assembled in the Grodno area, entrained on the 25th September, and travelled to France *via* Lyck—Graudenz—Berlin—Hannover—Minden—Cologne—Aachen—Liége—Namur—Douai, arriving on the 1st October. The 38th Division was then put into line in the sector south of the Oise, and, with the 54th Division, on its left, formed a temporary XI. Army Corps.

1916.   The division held this sector, in which it was not seriously engaged, until early in May, 1916, when it was relieved by the 113th Division. On the 11th May, the 38th Division entrained in the Tergnier area and was transported to the Verdun front. It came into line on the 13th May on the left bank of the Meuse, in the sector of Côte 304, where it relieved the 4th Division. During the five months the division held this sector it was engaged in a great deal of hard fighting and suffered severely. It was relieved on the 10th October by the 13th Division. The casualties reported officially for this fighting were 5,552 (for 9 battalions).

The 38th Division entrained on the 12th October and was transported to the Somme front by Carignan—Sedan—Mezières—Hirson—Avesnes—Valenciennes—Bouchain—Cambrai, detraining near Bullecourt. It came into line on the 21st-22nd October in the Thiepval-Grandcourt sector, and relieved the 28th Reserve Division. The division suffered severely in this sector and had to be withdrawn after three weeks in line. It was relieved on the 13th November by the 223rd Division and transferred to the coast of Flanders to rest and refit. The 38th Division entrained on the 15th November, and travelled *via* Aubigny-au-Bac—Douai—Lille—Roubaix—Courtrai—Iseghem—Roulers—Thourout to Bruges. It was then distributed between Ostend and the Belgian-Dutch frontier, and for a month was employed in guarding the coast and the frontier in that area.

On the 19th December, the division returned to the Somme front. It entrained at Ostend and travelled *via* Thourout—Roulers—Lille—Orchies—St. Amand—

1917.   Valenciennes—Cambrai to Ecoust-St.-Mein. During January, 1917, elements of the division were sent up to support the 56th Division in the area north of Courcelette and the 14th Bavarian Division south-west of Serre. On the 25th January, the whole division came into line and replaced the 14th Bavarian Division. Early in March, it retired to the Puisieux area, and was then replaced by the 18th Division. The division was not seriously engaged during this period. It reappeared again on the 17th March in the Beugny—Bertincourt sector, and relieved the 4th Guard Division, which had suffered severely in the early stages of the retreat to the Hindenburg Line. The 38th Division continued to withdraw *via* Beaumetz and Doignies till it had reached its allotted sector of the Hindenburg position between Demicourt and Boursies, west of Cambrai, where it was finally relieved at the end of April by the 17th Division.

The 38th Division rested for short periods at Cambrai, Douai, Bellonne and Brebières, and on the 15th-16th May relieved the 4th Ersatz Division east of Arras, in the sector just north of the River Scarpe. On the 16th May, the division carried out a very costly counter-attack on the village of Roeux, in which the 95th Infantry Regiment alone lost 800 men. It was replaced on the 30th-31st May by the 238th Division and rested at Douai for a week.

On the 8th June, the 38th Division entrained at Flines, north-east of Douai, and was railed to Iseghem in Flanders, whence it went into billets in the Dadizeele—Gheluwe area. The division was probably intended as a reinforcement for the Wytschaete-Messines front, but, as the British attacks in this area were not continued after the original objectives were gained, it was not required and remained in reserve. When, however, towards the end of July, a British attack on a large scale from the direction of Ypres became imminent, the 38th Division was sent up, and relieved the 17th Division in the Hooge sector, east of Ypres, on the 27th July. In the three days prior to the attack, it suffered heavy losses from our shelling and reconnaissances in force, and on the 31st July met the full weight of the British assault. Owing to its heavy losses it was relieved on the 1st August and transferred to Antwerp to rest and refit. The 38th Division rested in this area until the end of August, when it was transferred to the Arras front. It entrained at Cappellen (north of Antwerp) on the 29th August, and travelled *via* Antwerp—Malines—Brussels—Mons—Valenciennes—Douai to Cantin, where it detained on the same day. On the 2nd September, it came into line in the Monchy-le-Preux sector (south of River Scarpe), and relieved the 17th Reserve Division. Although the division only held this sector for two months, it suffered severely from gas shell and harassing fire, and is said to have had over 1,000 casualties. It was relieved by the 24th Division on the 2nd November, and rested in the Douai area for a week, when it was again transferred to Flanders.

The 38th Division replaced the 41st Division in the Staden sector (north of Ypres) on the 19th November, and held this front until the 25th November, when it was again replaced by the 41st Division. After spending five days in reserve, it came into line north of Passchendaele, where it relieved the 199th Division. On the 3rd December, the British carried out a local attack in this area and inflicted serious losses on the division. The 94th Infantry Regiment suffered severely in the subsequent counter-attack it carried out. The 38th Division remained in this sector, alternating in line with the 2nd Guard Reserve Division, until the 19th December, when it was finally withdrawn to rest. After a month spent resting in the Bruges area, the division returned to the Flanders front, this time to the Staden sector, relieving

1918. the 41st Division on the 13th-14th January, 1918. It was itself relieved on the 4th-5th February by the 199th Division.

Uniform. The monogram on the shoulder-straps of the 94th Infantry Regiment, which was formerly " C.A.," is now " W.E.," the initials of General der Infanterie Wilhelm Ernst, Grand Duke of Saxony, who is Colonel-in-Chief of the 94th Infantry Regiment (Grossherzog von Sachsen).

General. The 38th Division is a good division. It has seen a great deal of fighting, and has usually acquitted itself well. The serious losses of the division after the fighting at Ypres at the end of July, 1917, affected, temporarily at any rate, the *moral* of the division.

The 38th Division is commanded by Lt.-Gen. Schultheiss.

NOTE ON THE 39th DIVISION.

Composition. The 39th Division is nominally recruited in the XV. Army Corps District (Alsace), but most of the units draw their drafts from other Army Corps Districts. The reason for this being that the Alsatians are not trusted, and, with few exceptions, were all drafted to units on the Eastern front.

The 39th Division originally comprised the 61st Infantry Brigade (126th and 132nd Infantry Regiments) and the 82nd Infantry Brigade (171st and 172nd Infantry Regiments). In March, 1915, this division was reconstituted on the three-regiment basis. The 171st Infantry Regiment was withdrawn to join the 115th Division, and the remaining three infantry regiments were grouped together in the 61st Infantry Brigade.

History, 1914. At the beginning of the war, the XV. Army Corps (30th and 39th Divisions) formed part of the Seventh German Army (von Heeringen), which advanced through the Northern Vosges, but failed to break through the defences of the Upper Moselle. Early in October, the Corps was transferred to the area north of Reims, where it remained for about a month. The Corps was then rushed up to Flanders, where it took part in the heavy fighting subsequent to the first battle of Ypres and took over the front between the Ypres—Menin road and the Ypres—Comines Canal.

1915. During the whole of 1915, the Corps was almost continually engaged in local fighting. In the battle which began on the 17th April round Hill 60 (south-east of Ypres), the 105th Infantry Regiment suffered particularly heavy casualties and lost a number of prisoners. The Corps took no active part in the second battle of Ypres, but advanced its line as far as Hooge, when the British forces withdrew to a shorter line after the battle. In July and August, heavy local fighting took place at Hooge, in which the 126th Infantry Regiment lost some prisoners.

1916. During January, 1916, the XV. Army Corps was gradually relieved south-east of Ypres by the XIII. Army Corps. Between the 23rd and 30th January, it entrained at Courtrai and travelled *via* Ath—Mons—Charleroi—Namur—Libramont—Arlon—Luxemburg to Aumetz and came into line in the Etain—Damloup sector, east of Verdun, on about the 20th February. It remained in line in this area for about eight months. Immediately upon its arrival on this front the XV.

Corps was engaged in the Verdun battle. At the outset, it was able to advance its line considerably in the Woëvre Plain, but was brought to a standstill when it had reached the Hauts de Meuse. The 105th Infantry Regiment (30th Division), which was in divisional reserve, was called upon to reinforce the III. Army Corps and took part in the attack on the Bois de Chauffour, in the Douaumont sector on the 26th February. During June and the following months, elements of the Corps were severely handled by the French in the fighting around Vaux Fort and the Thiaumont Work. The total casualties, admitted officially, for the 39th Division in the Battle of Verdun were 8,548.

Early in October, when the fighting on the Verdun front had practically come to a standstill, the XV. Corps was relieved by the 19th Ersatz Division. It entrained between the 3rd and 10th October at Baroncourt and came by Sedan and Hirson to the Valenciennes area. On the 25th-28th October, the Corps relieved the 1st and 2nd Bavarian Divisions in the Sailly-Saillisel sector north of the Somme. Bitter fighting took place here. The French drove the Corps from its positions, captured part of the village of Sailly-Saillisel and took about 390 prisoners of the 30th Division and 370 of the 39th Division. The Corps was withdrawn from the Somme about the middle of November and transferred to the area north of Verdun to rest and refit. The 39th Division was relieved on the 11th November by the 185th Division, and the 30th Division on the 18th November by the 27th Division.

The 39th Division went back into line again early in December, when it relieved the 13th Reserve Division in the Haudromont sector, north of Verdun. On the 15th December this division had to bear the brunt of the second French counter-offensive at Verdun. It suffered severely and lost a large number of prisoners. The 30th Division took the place of the 39th Division in this sector on the 21st December.

1917. When the 39th Division left the Verdun front, it was transferred to the Argonne, and relieved the 7th Reserve Division north of Ville-sur-Tourbe on the 9th January. It was not engaged in any fighting in this area. At the beginning of May, it was relieved by the 214th Division and transferred to the Loivre sector, north-west of Reims, where it relieved the Guard Ersatz Division on the 5th May. The division saw only very little fighting on this front, and, when it was withdrawn at the beginning of July, came out of line as a comparatively fresh division.

After a short period of rest, the 39th Division entrained at Wasigny and came viâ Cambrai to Aniche, relieving the 220th Division south-east of Arras on the 15th July. After five uneventful weeks in this sector it was replaced by the 49th Reserve Division, and proceeded to the Lens area. It acted as a reserve for this front at the end of August, but, as the fighting subsided soon after its arrival, it did not go into line until the middle of September. The Division relieved the 4th Guard Division north of Lens on about the 15th September and was in turn relieved by the 185th Division on about the 10th October.

From Lens, the 39th Division was sent to Flanders, and, on the 19th October, took over the sector west of Passchendaele. It was relieved by the 3rd Guard Division on the 26th October and came back into line in the same sector on the 30th October, relieving the 238th Division. On the 5th November it was relieved by the 11th Division and moved to the Becelaere sector, where it relieved the 36th Reserve Division on the 8th November. After an eight days' tour of duty in this sector it was relieved by the 36th Reserve Division and withdrawn from Flanders. The 39th Division saw heavy fighting about Passchendaele early in November and suffered heavy losses from artillery fire.

After a short period of rest, the 39th Division came into line in a quiet sector north of the La Bassée Canal, replacing the 234th Division on the 24th November. The division, which was not engaged in any fighting in this area, was relieved on

1918. the 26th February by the 44th Reserve Division and went to rest in the Lille area. On the 13th March, elements of the division carried out a raid south of Armentières in the sector of the 10th Ersatz Division.

General. The 39th Division can be classed among the good German divisions. It has fought consistently well throughout the war. During the early part of the war, when the division contained a large number of Alsatians, desertions were an almost daily occurrence, but after the battle of Verdun all Alsatians were withdrawn and sent to units on the Eastern front.

The 39th Division is commanded by Maj.-Gen. von Davans.

NOTE ON THE 40th DIVISION.

Composition. The 40th (4th Saxon) Division originally formed, with the 24th (2nd Saxon) Division, the XIX. (Second Royal Saxon) Army Corps, the headquarters of which are at Leipzig.

The 40th Division originally consisted of the 88th (7th Saxon) Infantry Brigade, comprising the 104th (5th Saxon) and 181st (15th Saxon) Infantry Regiments, and the 89th (8th Saxon) Infantry Brigade, comprising the 133rd (9th Saxon) and 134th (10th Saxon) Infantry Regiments. At the end of 1915, the 133rd Infantry Regiment was withdrawn to join the 24th Division, and the remaining three regiments were grouped in the 88th Infantry Brigade.

History.
1914. At the beginning of the war, the XIX. Corps formed part of the Third German Army under General von Hausen, which advanced through the Ardennes and took part in the battle of Dinant. In the subsequent wheel southwards, the XIX. Corps crossed the Marne near Chalons, and reached a point some way south of that town, where the German Army was compelled to retreat to the Aisne. In the "race for the sea" at the end of October, the XIX. Corps was transferred to the Sixth Army under the Crown Prince of Bavaria. It was engaged by our cavalry and the advanced guard of our III. Corps, and driven back on to the line between Ploegsteert Wood and Bois Grenier.

1915. During 1915 and the first half of 1916, the XIX. Corps as a whole was not seriously engaged. Elements of both its divisions were sent to reinforce threatened sectors of the front on various occasions, returning to the Corps sector between Ploegsteert Wood and Bois Grenier when their help was no longer required. Elements of the 24th Division were engaged at L'Epinette, east of Armentières, in January. In the battles of Neuve Chapelle, in March, and Festubert, in May and June, the division sent up reinforcements to support the VII. Corps.

1916. At the beginning of August, 1916, the XIX. Corps was transferred to the Somme front. The 40th Division went into line east of Pozières, relieving elements of the IX. Reserve Corps. It was engaged in severe fighting and suffered heavy losses. After spending about three weeks in line, the Corps was transferred to the Neuve Chapelle—La Bassée sector, but after six weeks' rest returned to the Somme front. The 40th Division relieved the 6th Bavarian Reserve Division south-west of Bapaume on the 14th October, and remained in line for three weeks. Early in November, the XIX. Corps was relieved by the Guard Reserve Corps, and returned to the St. Eloi-Messines front. The 40th Division went into line in the Messines sector, and relieved the 26th Division. The losses reported by the 40th Division in the Somme battle amounted to 6,127, or 68 per cent. of establishment.

1917. Prior to the British offensive at Arras, the 40th Division was relieved by the 2nd Division, and went to rest in the Renaix area. Elements of the 134th Infantry Regiment reinforced the 111th Division in the Givenchy-en-Gohelle sector, but were not seriously engaged. On the 23rd April, the 40th Division went into line again at Messines and relieved the 2nd Division.

When it became evident to the German Higher Command that a British offensive was imminent on the Wytschaete-Messines front, preparations were made to withdraw the Saxon elements in line in that area. The 40th Division was not relieved until the night of the 6th-7th June, when its place was taken by the 3rd Bavarian Division. It suffered extremely heavy losses in the preliminary bombardment to the Messines battle, and on the 7th June, the day of the attack, left 462 prisoners in the hands of the British. It rested in the Bruges area until the 19th July, when it entrained at Steenbrugge, and came to Thourout. On the 22nd July, the division came into line north of Ypres, and took over one regimental sector of the 49th Reserve Division on its left and relieved part of the 19th Landwehr Division on its right. In this sector the division suffered severely from artillery fire, and on the 31st July was engaged by the Franco-British attack. Only part of the divisional front was involved in the attack, so that the losses of the division were not excessive. It was replaced on the 14th August by the 119th Division, and, on the 20th August, took over the Itancourt-Alaincourt sector (south of St. Quentin) from the 208th Division.

After almost two months' rest in this quiet sector, the 40th Division was relieved by the 4th Guard Division and returned to the Ypres front, where it relieved the 119th Division and elements of the 58th Division, north of Bixschoote, on the 16th October. The division was seriously engaged in the French attack, which took place on the 27th October, and lost the village of Merckem. It was relieved on the 27th October by the 8th Bavarian Reserve Division, and transferred to the Russian front, where it relieved the 123rd Division in the Lake Narotch area early in November.

General. The 40th Division is not a unit of good fighting quality. Its *moral*, like that of most Saxon units, is poor. During 1915 and the first half of 1916, when in the Armentières sector, its attitude was entirely passive. The division fought fairly well on the Somme. In 1917, its *moral* deteriorated considerably, and cases of desertion were frequent. At Ypres the division showed very little fight, and usually evacuated its position when menaced by a serious attack.

The 40th Division is commanded by Maj.-Gen. Meister.

NOTE ON THE 41st DIVISION.

Composition. The 41st Division is recruited in the XX. Army Corps District (East Prussia), which comprises the towns of Allenstein, Lyck, Soldau, Osterode, Marienburg, Elbing, Lötzen.

The 41st Division originally consisted of the 72nd Infantry Brigade (18th and 59th Infantry Regiments), and the 74th Infantry Brigade (148th and 152nd Infantry Regiments). During May, 1915, the 59th Infantry Regiment was withdrawn to form part of a new 101st Division, and the remaining three regiments were grouped in the 74th Infantry Brigade.

History, 1914. The XX. Army Corps, consisting of the 37th and 41st Divisions, on taking the field in August, 1914, was engaged in its own area, East Prussia, and formed part of the Eighth German Army under von Hindenburg. With this army it took part in the battle of Tannenburg on the 30th August, and in the battle of Lötzen on the 9th September. Towards the end of September the XX. Corps was transferred by rail to Upper Silesia, which was being threatened by the Russian advance. Here the Corps joined the Ninth German Army under von Mackensen, and took part in the second German offensive. It was engaged in the fighting about Radom on the 6th October and took part in the advance on Warsaw and subsequent retreat. During December and January the Corps formed part of the Tenth German Army, and was engaged in the heavy fighting that took place south of the Bzura.

1915. The XX. Army Corps left Russian Poland in February, 1915, and returned to East Prussia, where it was engaged in the battle of the Mazurian Lakes which culminated in the withdrawal of the Russians from German territory. In June, the XX. Army Corps was broken up, and the 41st Division was transferred to the Baltic area, participating in the advance on the Riga—Dvinsk front. When the fighting had died down, the division settled down in a quiet sector opposite Jacobstadt.

1916. The 41st Division remained in this area until October, 1916, when it was relieved by the 105th Division, and transferred to Transylvania. It travelled *via* Shavli—Vilna—Grodno—Warsaw—Breslau—Kattowitz—Temesvar to Petroseni. The division was first identified in the heavy fighting which took place at the beginning of November for the possession of the Vulcan Pass. Later, when it had entered Rumania, it was engaged south of Ploiesti, between Buzeu and Rimnicu, and, early in January, 1917, captured Slobozia and Rotesti.

1917. When the German advance had been brought to a standstill on the Sereth, the 41st Division was withdrawn and transferred to France. It entrained on the Sereth on the 27th January, and travelled through Styria and South Germany, detraining at Audun-le-Roman on the 12th February. The division remained in reserve in Woëvre until April, and, when the French offensive on the Aisne opened, was transferred to the Sissonne area as a reserve. It came into line in the Hurtebise sector (Craonne area) on the 27th May, relieving the 9th Division, and carried out a series of partly successful, but extremely costly counter-attacks. The 41st Division was relieved by the 5th Reserve Division on the 25th June, and, after a few days' rest replaced the 20th Division south of Ripont in Champagne. It was not seriously engaged in this sector and was withdrawn from line early in November as a comparatively fresh division.

The 41st Division entrained at Amagne on the 6th November and travelled *via* Charleville—Hirson—Aulnoye—Ghent—Deynze to the Lichtervelde area, where it detrained, and relieved the 27th Division in the Staden sector (north of Ypres) on the 10th November. It remained in this sector, without being seriously engaged, **1918.** until the 14th January, alternating with the 38th Division. After five weeks' rest in the Bruges area, the division came into line north of Passchendaele, where it replaced the 2nd Guard Reserve Division and remained until the 4th March, when it was relieved by the 38th Division and went to rest at Tourcoing.

General. The 41st Division, which made its first appearance on the British front in November, 1917, appears to be a moderately good division. During the campaign in Rumania in 1916 the division was mentioned on several occasions in the German official communiqué, and in the fighting at Hurtebise in 1917 was praised for the vigour with which it had carried out certain attacks. It is composed of west and east Prussians, who usually give a good account of themselves.

The 41st Division is commanded by Maj-Gen. Gräser.

NOTE ON THE 42nd DIVISION.

Composition. The 42nd Division is recruited in the Saarbrücken area (XXI. Corps District), but also drawns upon the VII. Corps District (Westphalia) for reinforcements. At the outbreak of war the 42nd Division comprised the 59th Infantry Brigade (97th and 138th Infantry Regiments) and 65th Infantry Brigade (17th and 131st Infantry Regiments). In the spring of 1915, the 97th Infantry Regiment was withdrawn to form part of the 108th Division, and the three remaining regiments were grouped under the staff of the 65th Infantry Brigade.

History, 1914. The XXI. Corps (comprising the 31st and 42nd Divisions), on mobilization, was included in the Sixth German Army under the Crown Prince of Bavaria, which invaded French Lorraine, but was held up in front of Nancy. When, after the retreat to the Aisne, the Sixth Army was transferred from Lorraine to Artois, the 42nd Division, with its sister division, was transferred to the Second Army in Picardy. The 42nd Division was engaged in the Vermandovillers area south of the River Somme.

1915. In February, 1915, the two divisions of the XXI. Corps were transferred to the Eastern front and allotted to the Eighth (later Tenth) Army under von Eichhorn on the East Prussian frontier. The Corps entrained in the Chaulnes area, and travelled *via* St. Quentin—Hirson—Charleville—Longuyon—Diedenhofen to Lipsk. In the great summer offensive of 1915, the Tenth Army, on the left flank, maintained a passive attitude until after the capture of Warsaw at the end of July; it then advanced rapidly, taking Kovno and Vilna, but was brought to a standstill in the autumn just east of the latter place. When the front became stationary the 42nd Division took up a position in the Postavi area, north-east of Vilna.

In June, 1917, the 42nd Division was withdrawn from line, and early in July was transferred to France, returning to Russia, however, before it was engaged; it took part in the Austro-German offensive in Galicia, which forced the Russians to evacuate practically the whole of Galicia. When fighting in this area had died down, the division was transported north, and, early in September, took part in the battle which culminated in the capture of Riga. At the beginning of October, it was transferred to Libau, and embarked on the 11th for the Island of Oesel, the whole of which it had captured by the end of the month. It was relieved by Landsturm formations and returned to Libau on the 1st November, whence it was transferred to the Kovel area, relieving the 107th Division on the 9th November. The division suffered very few casualties in the fighting at Riga and on Oesel. On the 20th December, after the armistice between the Russians and Germans had been concluded, the 42nd Division entrained at Kovel for France, travelling *via* Warsaw—Thorn—Posen—Leipzig—Dortmund—Cologne—Aachen—Herbesthal—Louvain—Brussels to Ascq,

where it detrained on the 28th December. After a short rest in the Lille area, the 42nd Division came into line opposite Armentières, relieving the 4th Division on the 23rd January.

The 42nd Division, which has not been engaged on the Western front since 1914, was engaged in the three important operations on the Russian front in 1917, and should be a useful division in open warfare. From the indications received since its return to the Western front, the *moral* of the men does not appear to be good.

The 42nd Division is commanded by Maj.-Gen. Buchholz.

www.ingramcontent.com/pod-product-compliance
Lightning Source LLC
Chambersburg PA
CBHW081543090426
42741CB00014BA/3248